SYLVIA CALDWELL

Arise: Your Road to Wholeness After Sexual Trauma

Your Healing Journey

Caldwell *WellSpring*
PUBLISHING

First published by Caldwell Wellspring Publishing 2026

Disclaimer

This book is for educational and informational purposes only and is not intended as medical, psychological, or therapeutic advice, diagnosis, or treatment. The author shares personal experience, perspective, and educational insight to support individual healing. Readers are responsible for their own well-being, choices, and application of the material.

First edition

This book was professionally typeset on Reedsy.
Find out more at reedsy.com

This book is dedicated to Abba—
The One who pursued me relentlessly,
who never let me go,
who loved me even when I cursed You and wanted to take my own life.
You protected me and hovered over me when I could have gone straight into darkness.
You gave me strength through every dark night.
You healed me.
You healed my family.
You gave me life.
You saved me.
You sent Your beloved Son so I could be fully free.
You are my entire life,
and my story is for Your glory.

"He heals the brokenhearted and binds
up their wounds."

– Psalm 147:3

Contents

Foreword

"Never give up."

This is the phrase that keeps coming to mind when I ponder what to write for this foreword. Of all my wife Sylvia's qualities—beauty, wisdom, zeal, love, compassion, and dedication—the one that has carried her through healing and restoration is her tenacity to never give up.

I've watched her walk through many highs and lows on her healing journey. I've seen her on the mountaintop as she received revelation from God, and I've seen her in the darkest valley as she cried out her heart before that breakthrough came. She never gave up.

Watching Sylvia's radical bravery and raw authenticity actually allowed me to open up about sexual abuse that happened to me in adolescence—something I had told no one for forty years of my life. I have watched her in the days of such deep depression she could barely leave a room, when she couldn't go to the bathroom by herself, when anxiety attacks made her think she might die. And I have watched her transform—from a trapped girl who didn't know her worth and reenacted her trauma—into a daughter of the King who walks in authority and has brought shalom peace into places that were once torment.

I have also witnessed Sylvia help countless women of all ages. She loves with her whole heart. I've seen many transformed, and I've also seen some betray her—yet she loves them all deeply and intentionally. I have watched her pray and fast for people who have deeply hurt her. I have been encouraged again and again by the love she radiates. She lives and breathes the presence of God.

Sylvia is not perfect, but she is quick to learn, quick to repent, and committed to walking out the truth that iron sharpens iron. When the Holy Spirit convicts her, she doesn't offer a shallow apology—she turns and walks in a new direction. You can trust Sylvia because the thing she cares about most is being close to God.

She has also helped me, on numerous occasions, process my own abuse, hurt, and pain. I can say firsthand that she is a sincere and compassionate guide. I've seen her help other women through their trials, and each time there is life on the other side.

You're not getting a guaranteed, seven-step program for healing "or your money back!" with this book. What you are getting is a guide from someone who has been in the trenches, survived the battles, and won the war. And that's what it takes to win the battles—the courage to show up day after day and fight for your freedom.

I'm honored to call Sylvia my wife, my friend, and the mother of our children. I'm proud of her compassion to help others with what she has learned, and I know this book will impact you, dear reader.

Sincerely,

Micah Caldwell

Sylvia has profoundly impacted my healing journey from sexual trauma and the deep shame surrounding it, as well as so many other broken places in my life. She wasn't afraid to walk with me through old trauma and intense subjects that no one else was willing to talk about. Where others avoided the hard conversations, she leaned in with truth, wisdom, and compassion.

When I met her, I had been an addict for eight years. I had been sexually abused and was living in prostitution. I felt defined by my past and disconnected from who I truly was. Sylvia met me with unwavering love and gently reminded me of my identity as a daughter of Christ. Through her obedience to the Holy Spirit, she didn't just offer encouragement—she helped me confront wounds, break agreement with shame, and begin real healing.

More than anything, she helped me cultivate my own personal relationship with Abba Father and the Holy Spirit. She didn't position herself as the source of answers; she pointed me back to God again and again. The day I surrendered my life to Jesus marked a turning point, and I have never been the same. Today, I am a full-time missionary, falling more in love with Jesus every single day.

Having experienced her wisdom, courage, and deep love for God firsthand, I know this book will help others step into freedom, face what feels too painful to name, and discover true restoration in Christ.

-Bailey Mullinax

Sylvia is uniquely gifted at instantly connecting with others and leaving people feeling encouraged in the midst of some of life's most chaotic or tragic situations. She has an uncanny ability to connect with women and girls of different walks of life, ages, and cultures. Her life story is a powerful testament to the transforming power of Jesus Christ and the way He can bring wholeness out of brokenness. God has saved Sylvia through some very dark, troubling circumstances, and it is a joy to watch

Him use her story of redemption to help other girls and women find healing and restoration.

–Haley H.

I was raised in the church and have always been surrounded by strong Christian women in my community, but I have never met someone like Sylvia! She immediately challenged my faith and continually helps me seek the Lord in my everyday life. The way she lives her life is truly a testament to the powerful redemption she's experienced. She brings people into her walk and genuinely introduces them to Christ's love. She has opened my eyes to different ways God can communicate and how eager He is to have an engaged relationship with us. Sylvia's heart is beautiful, and I am so thankful to have her in my life.

–Josie G.

Preface

Dear Reader,

If you are holding this book, there is a reason.

Maybe you are exhausted from carrying something no one else can see. Maybe you have learned how to function, smile, serve, lead, or survive while parts of your heart still feel fractured. Or maybe you are just beginning to realize that what happened to you did not simply "stay in the past."

I want you to know something before you turn another page: you are not too broken, too complicated, too far gone, or too ashamed for full restoration.

This book was not written from theory. It was born from years of walking through my own healing journey and sitting with others in the sacred, tender spaces of theirs. I have witnessed what happens when old trauma is no longer managed but surrendered. I have seen what God does when we allow Him into the places we once tried to seal shut.

For a long time, I believed healing meant learning how to cope better. I thought freedom meant minimizing the impact of what I had survived. But the Lord gently showed me that He never intended for us to merely manage our wounds — He intended to restore us.

ARISE was written to challenge the belief that trauma defines you. It was written to confront the lie that shame has the final word. It was written to lead you beyond worldly methods and into a biblical understanding of wholeness — spirit, soul, and body.

As you read, you may feel things you have not allowed yourself to feel in a long time. You may encounter resistance, fear, or even doubt. That is okay. Healing often begins at the edge of discomfort. You are not weak for feeling it — you are brave for staying.

My prayer is not that you would simply admire these pages, but that you would encounter Abba Father within them. That you would hear the gentle voice of the Holy Spirit guiding you. That you would discover for yourself the identity that trauma tried to steal.

Take your time. Breathe. You are not behind. You are not disqualified. You are not alone.

There is more for you than survival.

There is wholeness.

With love,

Sylvia

Before You Begin

Before you start this book, know this:

You were never meant to heal alone.

The pages ahead are powerful. They will stir things. They will awaken truth. They may uncover places in your story that have been buried for a long time.

And while you can absolutely walk through this journey on your own, there is another way.

You can choose to go through Arise inside the Group Coaching Experience — where we move chapter by chapter, side by side. In that space, we:

- Walk through each chapter together
- Process the activations live
- Receive teaching, guidance, and prayer
- Heal in safe, intentional community
- Build life long friendships

This is sacred work. And sacred work is strengthened in community.

If you feel the nudge to not just read this book — but to fully step into it — you are invited.

Scan the QR code below to learn more and join the Arise Group Coaching Experience.

Connected is protected.

And you do not have to do this alone. See QR Code on next page!

IT'S Your Turn
To Heal

Acknowledgments

This book is also dedicated to my dear friend, Carole Anderson—
 a true daughter of the King.

Your wisdom and love have echoed through my soul for more than fifteen years.

I am forever grateful for your patience and generosity.

You loved and prayed for the broken girl who sat on the couch in your office all those years ago.

You planted seeds in me that will last for a thousand generations.

Carole, you are a beloved daughter of the Most High— beautiful inside and out.

Anyone who crosses your path is blessed to know you.

To my beautiful family. Thank you for sowing me into the Kingdom. Team Caldwell, you are irreplaceable, my entire inspiration for healing. Together, we have transformed a bloodline. We will all reap a plentiful harvest of abundance.

To Amanda, Tonya & Jen! Thank you for being friends who held my arms up when I could barely breathe, for always speaking iron sharpens iron, and for holding me accountable for this book. You have helped sow me into the Kingdom, and I pray you reap a plentiful harvest in return!

Introduction

Let me be clear: this book is a roadmap for your healing journey, based on my own experience overcoming trauma and finding purpose. I write as someone who has faced resistance in sharing this message, but I know how important it is. Every step I take to help you heal comes with challenges—times when I feel unqualified, broken, or overwhelmed.

Here's what I've learned: this pushback is **proof**. It shows that the message I live by has the power to set captives free. And that captive includes you.

Many, many women I've spoken with share the same struggle: feeling trapped, isolated, and powerless in the wake of sexual trauma. They wonder if healing is possible, or if life will always feel shadowed by fear, shame, and pain. Without intentional steps, trauma continues to steal joy, intimacy, peace, and purpose. It will not improve on its own. But here's the good news: **God healed me, and He will do it for you, too.**

Sharing our testimony is a blow the enemy cannot recover from. It is David's stone flung straight into the forehead of the giant. Every time a survivor opens her mouth and tells the truth about what God has done, hell loses territory. The enemy can tempt, rattle, accuse, intimidate—but he cannot undo a testimony. He cannot un-resurrect what God has healed. He cannot erase the places where God has redeemed the story.

I am moving forward. I'm walking past the rattling doors

and choosing the light. You need to know this: your obedience affects someone else's life—not as pressure, but as purpose. Your freedom will inspire courage in another. Your healing will guide someone else. Your voice will become a weapon. Together, step by step, story by story, we will reclaim what trauma tried to steal.

What if I told you healing isn't just possible—it's a journey designed to lead you into your greatest purpose?

My name is Sylvia Caldwell, and I've dedicated my life to helping women reclaim their lives after trauma, using a faith-centered approach rooted in hope, healing, and purpose.

There was a chapter in my life so dark that sometimes I forget it ever existed. I was broken and tormented. A spirit of trauma followed me like a shadow I couldn't escape. It seeped into every part of me and showed up as what the world labels depression, anxiety, and, at times, even bipolar disorder. I was trapped in a cycle of trauma reenactment. I was drowning in addiction, consumed by sorrow, and buried in shame. Nothing in the world could fill the void in my soul.

Then something changed. It was shortly after I made the decision to believe in Jesus that I felt the faintest glimmer of hope—no bigger than a mustard seed. The Holy Spirit whispered that this could not be the end of my story. There had to be more.

From that moment, God began to work in me, guiding me through a journey of restoration and renewal, one step at a time. He didn't rush me but patiently healed wounds I didn't know existed. The process wasn't easy or instant. But it was real and life-changing.

And I want to show you that **the same path, the same hope, and the same healing are possible for you.** I've walked it. I've searched for answers. I've found what works—and now I've turned it into a **proven approach that you can follow step by step**. It is possible to get the results you are dreaming of. I did it—and so can you.

This book is a reflection of my healing journey, but it's not just about me—it's about you. It's a guide to help you walk through your own healing process. It's an invitation to believe that, no matter how broken you feel, no matter how deep your pain runs, **there is hope**. You are not alone, and your story isn't over.

Maybe you're reading this because you're carrying wounds that no one can see. Maybe the pain feels so overwhelming that you wonder if healing is possible, or you've tried to move on, but something keeps pulling you back into the past. These are the struggles I hear from countless women—they feel stuck and unsure if life will ever feel whole again. I want you to know this: **you are not beyond healing.** The same God who walked with me through my darkest moments is ready to walk with you. Healing is not about forgetting or pretending the past didn't happen. It's about breaking free from its grip so you can step into the life God has for you.

This book is an invitation. It's a road map. It's a hand reaching out to say, *You don't have to do this alone.* Together, we will walk through the process of healing—one step at a time. Not by rushing through the pain, but by allowing God to bring restoration in His perfect way.

The biggest part of your healing will come through **clarity.** It's about understanding what has truly kept you stuck and what it takes to break free. Mainstream counseling, self-help movements, and even holistic psychology often offer valuable tools. But they often miss the **one thing that brings complete healing**.

Healing is not singular. It is a **trinity**. The only way to heal from sexual trauma is to restore your **spirit, soul, and body**. When these three areas align, research suggests it can impact up to **seven generations**. That means your choice to heal doesn't just change your life. It shifts the legacy of those who come after you.

Let me make something clear: you are **not alone**. Sexual abuse is a pervasive issue affecting countless individuals:

- **Prevalence:** Approximately 1 in 9 girls and 1 in 53 boys under the age of 18 experience sexual abuse or assault at the hands of an adult.
- **Gender Disparity:** 82% of all victims under 18 are female.
- **Age Vulnerability:** Females aged 16–19 are four times more likely than the general population to be victims of rape, attempted rape, or sexual assault.

And the impact extends far beyond the moment of abuse:

- **Suicide Risk:** Rape victims are 13 times more likely than non-crime victims to have attempted suicide.
- **Substance Abuse:** Rape is strongly linked to increased substance use as survivors attempt to cope with the trauma.

The world has been corrupted by darkness. Abuse is one of the enemy's greatest tools to keep people bound. Many who have suffered as you have been given worldly diagnoses—depression, anxiety, PTSD, addiction, even psychosis. In reality, so much of what the world calls a disorder is **actually a wound that needs healing**.

And healing is possible.

In this book, I am giving you a road map—one I wish I had

when I was lost, broken, and searching for answers. It would have saved me years of suffering. I would have paid millions of dollars to have it in my hands.

But today, I'm handing it to you.

This is your chance to step into healing. To reclaim your freedom. To break the cycle of pain that has held you captive for far too long. And together, through God's guidance and a proven approach, we will walk the path to restoration—**one step at a time**.

As you read this introduction, I feel like I know you all on the other side of this book. I sit in a coffee shop writing this, and somehow, I feel like you are right here with me. I don't want to ramble on forever in this introduction, so I want to leave you with a glimpse of what to expect in this book.

The ARISE framework is truly special. It wasn't just written by me, but inspired by God. It starts simply, focusing on your vision—your "why" for healing and your dream for life after healing. Once we explore that, I'll guide you step by step to bridge the gap between your "why" and your dream. What brought you to want healing from the abuse and trauma you faced? And what does your dream life look like beyond the daily torment? This book covers nine phases in a strategic order, and each one is essential. If you're like me and sometimes skip the last chapters, know that your freedom depends on the ninth phase. It's the arsenal in your tool belt against the enemy, but you can't have that arsenal without completing the earlier phases—they all work together.

So, friend, I know this feels hard, scary, and exciting all at once. But I invite you to be brave—commit fully to reading and applying the principles in this book. Take each step knowing your healing depends on your willingness to keep going. I believe in you, I pray for you, and I know your healing is waiting on the other side of these pages. It's your turn—don't give up. Do whatever it takes to get through this book. Your breakthrough starts with your next step—start now.

I like to use this analogy.

Imagine you've planned your dream vacation. Really, picture it. For me, it would be Greece—crystal-clear waters, ancient architecture, warm sun on my skin. People walking through village streets, sharing meals made from their gardens. Fresh feta, spanakopita, locals playing soccer, and me jumping in to play alongside them.

Now imagine I'm at home preparing for this trip. I buy new clothes, pick out accessories, get my hair done—everything needed for the journey. Finally, it's time to board the plane.

Flying isn't my favorite. I don't love being out of control of something so big, but I trust the pilot. Once we're in the air, we hit heavy turbulence—violent shaking, uncomfortable moments, fear rising in my body.

At that point, I have a choice.

I could panic, open the emergency exit, and jump—seriously injuring myself or even dying.

But of course, I don't do that.

Instead, I stay seated. I trust that even though the ride is rough, the pilot knows where we're going. I pray and believe the turbulence is not the destination. I know what's waiting on the other side is worth it.

This is a picture of what it takes to move through all nine phases of this book.

When the turbulence hits, don't give up.

Do not jump from the plane.

Chaos only leads to one place: destruction and death. You've already faced enough hardship and chaos to last a lifetime. Don't give in when resistance comes. You've been called to walk this journey and to overcome the chaos, not be consumed by it. Peace means breaking the power behind the spirit of chaos, and that's exactly what we will do.

And if you're wondering *why* God would call you, let me give you a spoiler alert for the chapters ahead.

God did not cause the abuse you endured. It was never His will for your life. He is not passive about what happened to you—He is angry at the enemy, committed to justice, and deeply invested in your healing. More than anything, He wants you to experience your salvation—**sozo**—a word that means complete healing: spirit, soul, and body. (We'll unpack this fully as we go.) Not everyone reading this is going to be called to help others heal from sexual abuse and trauma, don't get freaked out. But everyone here is called a daughter of the king. Maybe your healing looks like fullness in relationships, being a mom not bound by torment, living beyond depression, painting a picture, baking, or running your own business. No matter what your call looks like, healing is essential for your freedom.

The next few paragraphs will address some of the most common questions people carry at this stage of the journey. After that, it's time to fasten your seat belt—and begin to fly.

1. What makes this book different from other trauma recovery resources?

The Arise: Your Road to Wholeness After Sexual Trauma, Your Journey to Healing and Freedom book distinguishes itself from other trauma recovery resources by offering an approach that challenges the common misconceptions of trauma recovery in the world. While mainstream psychology and self-help methods often focus on managing trauma, ARISE goes beyond coping techniques by providing a biblical solution for full restoration—spirit, soul, and body. It recognizes that trauma is spiritual in nature and cannot be fully healed through psychological methods alone. The book encourages individuals to confront the spiritual roots of trauma, such as fear, rejection, and control, and apply God's Word and power to break these strongholds. Instead of just providing tools for survival, the book equips readers to experience complete healing through Christ's transformative power, offering a path to freedom that transcends secular methods. This approach not only empowers the individual but also honors God's design for restoration, offering a new identity in Christ rather than a "new way to cope."

2. Why is healing the spirit, soul, and body necessary instead of just focusing on one area?

Healing the spirit, soul, and body is crucial because, according to God's Word, each part of us is connected and affects the others. The world often focuses only on one aspect, such as the mind (psychological approaches) or the body (physical therapies), leaving other areas unhealed. For instance, self-help books may teach mental techniques, but they often neglect the spiritual strongholds that keep a person trapped in cycles of trauma. The ARISE book takes a holistic approach, addressing all three areas because God designed us to be whole beings. Trauma affects the soul and spirit first, and without addressing those deep-rooted issues, physical healing is only partial. By aligning the mind, body, and spirit with God's purpose, true restoration can take place. As 1 Thessalonians 5:23 says, "And the very God of peace sanctify you wholly; and I pray God your whole spirit and soul and body be preserved blameless..." Healing is not just about managing the symptoms of trauma but about transformation in all areas. Without this holistic view, we are left with fragmented healing, unable to walk fully in the freedom God has designed for us.

3. How does this book reflect God's design for restoration rather than just human methods of coping?

The ARISE book reflects God's design for restoration by emphasizing deliverance from spiritual strongholds and breaking the cycles of fear, control, and rejection—not just coping mechanisms or temporary solutions. The world's approach to trauma often revolves around managing the symptoms, sometimes through medication, therapy, or emotional coping skills. While these methods may offer some relief, they don't bring lasting freedom or true healing. ARISE offers a biblical blueprint for restoration that centers on the power of the Holy Spirit and God's Word. It teaches readers to break free from the spirit of fear (which often manifests as trauma, PTSD, and anxiety) and walk in the freedom provided by Christ. As John 8:36 states, "If the Son therefore shall make you free, ye shall be free indeed." Unlike the world's methods, which can leave individuals stuck in trauma, this approach focuses on full restoration through spiritual healing, the renewing of the mind, and alignment with God's truth. The ARISE book recognizes that healing is not about human strength or self-reliance but about surrendering to God's power and purpose for wholeness. Through this biblical process, readers can experience a true transformation—physically, emotionally, and spiritually.

This approach integrates the spiritual, emotional, and physical aspects of healing while also addressing the misconceptions that trauma is something that can only be coped with or managed. ARISE takes the reader beyond worldly methods into a biblical understanding of full restoration.

Because before true healing begins, the heart often wrestles with hidden fears—fear of revisiting pain, fear of change, and even fear of discovering who one might be without the wounds that have long shaped identity. The most common questions people carry as they stand at the edge of healing are often these:

1. Fear of the Unknown

- Fear: "What if I open old wounds that are too painful to deal with?"

It's natural to fear facing painful memories—I was absolutely terrified of them—but God promises to be with us every step of the way. In Psalm 34:18, it says, "The Lord is close to the brokenhearted and saves those who are crushed in spirit." Healing may involve confronting difficult emotions or memories, but God's presence will provide comfort and strength. Restoration doesn't mean staying stuck in pain; it means walking through the healing process with God's grace and peace, knowing that He will not leave us in the dark but will lead us to freedom.

2. Fear of Disappointment or Failure

- Fear: "What if I try to heal, but I don't see any change? What if I fail again?"

Usually, when this thought comes up, it is the enemy trying to plant despair and keep you stuck in a mindset that feels normal. Healing is a process, and it's not always immediate. But God has a plan for each person's healing, and His Word assures us that His timing is perfect. In Philippians 1:6, it says, "Being confident of this, that he who began a good work in you will carry it on to completion until the day of Christ Jesus." God does not fail, and He is faithful to finish the work He has started in us. Every step forward, no matter how small, is a victory.

3. Fear of Losing Control

- Fear: "What if this healing process takes me places I'm not ready to go, or I lose control over my emotions?"

You are not alone in this thought; many women share this feeling. It's common to feel like healing might strip us of control, especially when we've been in control for so long out of fear or survival instincts. However, God is the ultimate authority, and surrendering to Him is the only way to find true peace and restoration. In Proverbs 3:5-6, God invites us to trust Him fully: "Trust in the Lord with all your heart and lean not on your own understanding; in all your ways submit to him, and he will make your paths straight." Surrendering control to God does not lead to chaos; it leads to peace, freedom, and restoration in His perfect plan.

4. Fear of Facing Spiritual Struggles (e.g., fear of demonic oppression or spiritual warfare)

- Fear: "What if I have to face spiritual strongholds or demonic oppression as I heal?"

Spiritual warfare is real, but God is greater. Healing often involves breaking free from spiritual strongholds like fear, rejection, or control, which can be rooted in the enemy's schemes. However, we are not fighting alone. James 4:7 encourages us: "Submit yourselves, then, to God. Resist the devil, and he will flee from you." The authority of Christ gives us the power to break free from all spiritual oppression. 1 John 4:4 says, "You, dear children, are from God and have overcome them, because the one who is in you is greater than the one who is in the world." In Christ, we have victory over every attack of the enemy. In my personal experience—and you will hear more of my story in the next chapter—God does not forget those who experienced sexual abuse. He will not leave you alone and hurting as you walk through your healing process. He does not like that you were abused, and he certainly didn't allow it. He will be with you, and that's a PROMISE I can make you. And he will bring Justice.

5. Fear of Change or Transformation

- Fear: "What if I change so much that I don't recognize myself anymore, or I lose parts of who I am?"

Healing in Christ doesn't take away your identity; it restores it. God created you with a unique purpose, and true healing in Christ only helps you become more of who He intended you to be. Romans 8:29 tells us that God's plan is to "conform us to the image of His Son." Embracing God's design for our lives doesn't erase our identity; it restores and empowers it. The transformation that occurs through healing is a journey of growth, freedom, and restoration—not a loss of who you are, but a becoming more whole in Christ. As you return to your original design, you will feel lighter and lighter; the chains of trauma will break.

6. Fear of Vulnerability

- Fear: "What if I get hurt again or have to face rejection?"

Healing requires vulnerability, but God promises to protect us as we step into His healing process. In Psalm 34:19, it says, "The righteous person may have many troubles, but the Lord delivers him from them all." You may face moments of vulnerability, but God is faithful to protect and restore you. He understands your pain and will never reject you. Healing comes through trust, and God is trustworthy—so trustworthy with a giant AMEN. I have so many adventures and fun and comforting moments with Him—man, I wish you could look me in the eyes, sit for a while, and listen to the stories, because this may be very repetitive, but God will not fail, and this adventure is going to be sweet and fun and intentional. You are about to go on the most exciting journey of your life.

What Can You Expect to Gain from Finishing the ARISE Book?

I believe that if you read this and apply its truths, you will experience full healing and deliverance from the abuse you endured. Healing from sexual abuse, as the Bible describes, involves spiritual restoration and emotional healing, following God's design for your life. This journey can transform every part of you—spirit, soul, and body. You might be thinking, "Sylvia, this is the longest introduction ever." Please be patient—this is my first book. If I could go back and give myself advice before starting my healing journey 15 years ago, these would be the tips I'd give myself. So take note before you begin Chapter 1.

Commit to the Healing Process: It's a Journey Worth Taking

Healing is not an easy road, and I understand that stepping into the process of restoration might feel daunting. But I want to encourage you to take this step, knowing that God's plan for you is full of hope and wholeness. You might feel broken, unsure, or even fearful about what healing will look like, but I assure you that the journey of healing is one of freedom—freedom from the lies that have defined your past and freedom to live fully in the truth of who you are in Christ.

1. Trust in God's Power and Timing:

God is a faithful healer. His Word promises in Psalm 147:3 that He "heals the brokenhearted and binds up their wounds." He is not asking you to do this alone. Every step you take toward healing is a step He is walking with you. Trust His timing, and know that He is working all things together for your good, even when you can't see the full picture yet.

2. Embrace the Process, Even When It's Hard:

Healing involves confronting deep pain, but I promise you—

on the other side of that pain is wholeness. The process is worth it. As Romans 5:3-4 says, "We rejoice in our sufferings, knowing that suffering produces endurance, and endurance produces character, and character produces hope." Every moment of vulnerability, every tear, and every decision to move forward in faith is an investment in your future. You are not what happened to you; you are who God says you are—beloved, chosen, and empowered to heal.

3. Give Yourself Grace:

Healing doesn't mean perfection. It means progress. Be patient with yourself. God's grace covers every step of the way, and He will never condemn you for feeling imperfect or slow in the process. Take each day as it comes, and give yourself grace when setbacks happen. Philippians 1:6 assures us that "He who began a good work in you will carry it on to completion." Your journey of healing has already started, and God will finish what He has begun.

4. Let Go of the Lies and Embrace the Truth:

Throughout this book, you will confront lies that have been holding you back, and I encourage you to reject them with every fiber of your being. The truth is, you are more than your past. In John 8:32, Jesus promises, "Then you will know the truth, and the truth will set you free." The truth about your worth, your identity, and your future is found in God's Word, and it's time to live in the freedom of that truth.

5. Remember the Victory That Awaits You:

As you commit to the healing process, remember that this is not just about the healing of your wounds, but about the restoration of your purpose. You were created for more than survival; you were created to thrive and walk in the full life Christ has for you. You will emerge from this process stronger, more confident, and with a testimony that will bring glory to God.

Practical Steps for the Healing Journey

Here are some practical steps to get started on the healing journey with the ARISE framework:

- Pray Daily for Strength and Guidance:

Seek God's wisdom and strength every day as you move through the healing process. Pray for His peace and understanding to guide your steps.

- Set Small, Achievable Goals:

As you read through the ARISE book, set small, achievable goals for each phase. Celebrate your progress, no matter how small it may seem.

- Find a Support System:

Healing is not a solo journey. Surround yourself with people who will encourage, support, and pray for you along the way. You can find a link to our groups in the back of this book, or email livecalledwell@gmail.com and check my socials.

- Document Your Journey:

Keep a journal of your thoughts, prayers, and breakthroughs. This will help you track your progress and stay focused on your healing.

- Trust the Process:

Healing doesn't happen overnight, but every step is leading you closer to wholeness. Trust that God's timing is perfect and that He is at work in every part of your life.

1

Chapter 1: Awakening Your Why: The First Step to Healing

For years, I lived in survival mode—unsure who I was, where I was headed, or if true healing was possible. Everything changed when I found my why: the deeper purpose God intended beyond the pain.

I had always sensed there was more. Even in darkness, I felt the weight of something greater—a quiet but real pull toward life beyond trauma. As Ecclesiastes 3:11 says, "God set eternity in our hearts." Now, I see He planted purpose within me before I even understood it.

That purpose became clear during a defining season: when I became pregnant with my firstborn. As new life grew inside me, I awakened—something shifted. My past pain remained, but I glimpsed a strength greater than the pain.

Psalm 139:13 tells us that God knits us together in our mother's womb, and as I carried my child, I realized He had done the same for me—fearfully, wonderfully, and with intention. My story wasn't over. My why had been there all along, waiting to be uncovered.

Picture us as friends sharing coffee—if you know me, you know I hold nothing back.

Let me take you back fifteen years, to a cold winter day in Minnesota that marked the beginning of another chapter. I was in my mid-twenties—broke, confused, and uncertain about my future. Everything felt heavy, as if the world were pressing down. But in that moment, things started to shift.

I had just met Jesus Christ, and I knew in my heart that I would give my life to Him, but I didn't fully understand what that would require. I didn't yet realize that pre-marital sex shouldn't have been a compromise. I was still trapped in trauma and shame, my decisions clouded by the fear of rejection. In an attempt to fill that void, I gave my body away to my boyfriend, thinking it would somehow prove my worth and that I was loved.

During finals week, I thought the stress delayed my period. I'd been told I couldn't have children, so I didn't expect pregnancy. Standing outside in Minnesota's biting cold with classmates, surrounded by celebration, I suddenly felt: If I'm pregnant, I shouldn't be around this smoke.

Everything crashed together in that instant. The weight of the moment hit. I rushed to the store, heart pounding, hands shaking, cold biting my skin as I hurried through the snow. I bought a pregnancy test—not knowing it would change everything.

I took the test, and within seconds, two bright pink lines appeared. I was overwhelmed—flooded with so many emotions.

First, my boyfriend and I had just broken up.

Second, I was terrified. The memories of my past abuse made the thought of giving birth and breastfeeding almost impossible to face.

And third, I was full of shame. I was pregnant, unmarried, and had just started going to church. I was broke—emotionally and financially—struggling to find stability in my life.

But amid the chaos and fear, something began to stir within me: an awakening. This marked a transition from survival to seeking purpose, even in the face of uncertainty.

For the first time, I felt my why—the reason I was here, the deeper purpose behind it all. I knew I couldn't let my son grow up in the same brokenness. To change our lives, it was time to heal my soul, body, and spirit.

Before my why, I was stuck—wanting to heal but not knowing how. I call this my "half and half" journey: seeing the need for healing and help, but only halfway committed.

Halfway in was better than fully out, but still not enough. I wanted safety and wholeness, yet I remained in a victim mindset. That word can feel loaded, especially in Christian circles. But we all start somewhere. I was a victim, but I didn't need to stay in that identity. You'll know you're stuck because it affects your mind, will, and emotions.

A powerful verse that spoke to the deception and impact of trauma on my brain and soul was 2 Corinthians 10:5:

"We demolish arguments and every pretension that sets itself up against the knowledge of God, and we take captive every thought to make it obedient to Christ."

This verse shows us how easily our minds can be deceived by lies—how trauma can distort our perception of who we are and cause us to hold onto those lies. But it also tells us we don't have to stay stuck in those false beliefs. We can take those thoughts captive and make them obedient to Christ. Trauma can keep us trapped, but through Christ, we can renew our minds and align them with His truth.

And Romans 12:2 echoes that message:

"Do not conform to the pattern of this world, but be transformed by the renewing of your mind. Then you will be able to test and approve what God's will is—his good, pleasing, and perfect will."

Trauma doesn't have to define you. It doesn't have to control your thoughts. When we renew our minds in God's truth, we move away from the lies that have held us captive, and healing begins.

I couldn't admit the reality of my abuse for a long time. My biological father had hurt me, but it was painful to accept. I told myself it was someone else, unwilling to believe the truth.

For years, I avoided facing my pain. I looked for comfort in alcohol, food, shows, work, and chaotic relationships. These distractions numbed me but did not heal my emptiness.

Then, at 28, a turning point came: I found myself pregnant after that breakup. That's when everything shifted. Deep inside, I knew I wanted to parent differently, and suddenly, I was all in. I finally found my why. I wanted to heal, not just for me, but for the sake of my child. I wanted to be whole.

Have you ever felt stuck or unmotivated? Like the journey is just too long, too exhausting? I get it. I've been there. I felt your pain. I still feel it sometimes. But I'm here to tell you—you don't have to stay stuck. It's okay to pause and ask yourself, " What is your why? What brought you here to read this book?

I believe in you. I'm here to help. When healing seems out of reach, hold onto your purpose. Don't give up. I know it's hard, but it's worth every step. The freedom I've found on this journey is beyond what I imagined. As you move forward, let your why guide you—not just for hope tomorrow, but as the strength that shapes your story today. Remember, your journey is not over. Stay committed. The best is still to come, and you have the power to step into it.

Uncovering Your Why: Awakening Your Purpose

You're here—ready to discover your why. Congratulations on reaching this point of transformation. This is the first step toward a more purposeful, healed life.

Before you start digging into your why, I want you to pray. Holy Spirit, silence the voice of the enemy, Holy Spirit, silence any thoughts of mine that don't align with the word of God, and Holy Spirit, bind my mind to the mind of Christ.

Now, quick pause, if you are not a spirit-filled believer, let me explain something very important to you.

In many churches across America, the Gospel is often presented as a simple prayer — "Say this prayer and let Jesus into your heart." While the intent behind this message is not necessarily wrong, it can miss a crucial part of what Jesus truly offers. The Gospel is not just about asking Jesus to come into your heart; it is about dying to yourself and your old ways and giving your life to Him, including the life of abuse. It's about surrender. The message Jesus shared in the Gospels is far more radical and life-changing than simply asking for forgiveness. It's about laying down your own life so that you can be filled with the Holy Spirit and live a transformed life.

In Matthew 16:24, Jesus says, "If anyone would come after me, let him deny himself and take up his cross and follow me." This is not a prayer to say; it is a command to live by. He calls us to die to ourselves — to the control of our own souls and desires — and to give up the old way of living. It's in this process of surrender and transformation that we encounter the fullness of the Gospel. Jesus died for our sins so that we could live for Him, not simply to ask Him into our hearts, but to let Him be the Lord of our lives and receive the power to live that way through His

Spirit.

John 14:16-17 speaks about the Holy Spirit: "And I will ask the Father, and he will give you another Helper, to be with you forever, even the Spirit of truth, whom the world cannot receive, because it neither sees him nor knows him. You know him, for he dwells with you and will be in you." Jesus didn't just die and resurrect to give us a ticket to heaven. He left the Holy Spirit to guide, empower, and transform us in this life. We are meant to be filled with the Spirit and led by Him every day.

The Greek word for "Spirit" is pneuma ($\pi\nu\varepsilon\tilde{\upsilon}\mu\alpha$), which can be translated as "breath" or "wind." It refers to the life-giving force, the power of God that fills and transforms us. This isn't a passive experience — it's a dynamic, living relationship with the Creator of the universe. The Holy Spirit doesn't just live "in" us in the sense of being an occasional guest; He takes residence in us and begins the trans-formative work of making us more like Christ.

The Hebrew word for spirit is ruach (רוח), meaning "wind," "breath," or "spirit." In the Old Testament, it was the ruach of God that breathed life into Adam (Genesis 2:7) and the same ruach that empowered the prophets, kings, and leaders of Israel. The Holy Spirit, or ruach in Hebrew, is the life-breath that allows us to live according to God's will, leading us away from sin and into freedom.

I can speak from my own experience that my entire life changed when I became Holy Spirit-filled. Before that, I struggled, just as I mentioned before — trying to hold on to control of my life, thinking that if I prayed a specific prayer, I was saved, but still clinging to my own desires. My faith was stagnant. I still struggled with strongholds, the lies I had believed, and the traumas I hadn't healed from. But when I invited the Holy Spirit in — not just as a prayer but as a radical surrender — everything shifted. I wasn't just asking Jesus to be part of my life; I was laying down my life so He could take control. It wasn't about a ticket to heaven; it was about a transformed life right here, right now.

Only through the power of the Holy Spirit can strongholds be broken, and scales fall off our eyes. It's the Holy Spirit that enables us to truly walk in freedom, not through our own willpower or efforts, but through His strength and leading. Only He can heal wounds, renew our minds, and empower us to live out the new life that Jesus purchased for us on the cross. This is the transformation the Gospel brings. Without the Holy Spirit, there is no true transformation — just behavior modification.

Romans 8:11 reminds us: "If the Spirit of him who raised Jesus from the dead dwells in you, he who raised Christ Jesus from the dead will also give life to your mortal bodies through his Spirit who dwells in you." This is the resurrection power of the Holy Spirit that brings us from death to life — spiritually and practically.

We're not just called to believe in Jesus and "say a prayer"; we're called to die to our old selves, be raised up in Christ, and be filled with the Holy Spirit, who will equip us to live out the fullness of our salvation. Through Him, we are truly made new.

This is the Gospel — the Good News that's not about asking Jesus into your heart, but about being transformed by His power, dying to your own way, and living fully surrendered to Him, empowered by the Holy Spirit.

Back to the subject of finding your why...

I want to give you some encouragement and guidelines for discovering your why. Don't just stop at my example of I don't want my kid to have the same life I did. But dig deep. Find the emotions that are behind that.

Finding your why is an essential part of living a life that honors God, fulfills His purpose, and aligns with the divine design He has for each of us. Understanding your why isn't simply about finding a reason to keep going; it's about recognizing the unique role you play in God's larger, eternal plan, shaped by His design for your life, and that alone brings a reason to keep going. But this doesn't have to be complicated. My why is being a mom. It was quite enough. I didn't understand what I now do. But I was birthing an arrow in God's quiver, and that arrow I didn't want to dull or break.

Everything Has a Design and Purpose

The first step in discovering your why is acknowledging that everything in creation — including you — has a specific design and purpose. The Bible is clear that God doesn't create anything without intention. Psalm 139:13-14 declares, "For you formed my inward parts; you knitted me together in my mother's womb. I praise you, for I am fearfully and wonderfully made. Wonderful are your works; my soul knows it very well." This scripture reminds us that we were intricately and intentionally designed by God. There is a purpose behind every part of us, from our talents and passions to our struggles and triumphs.

This idea of design and purpose is woven throughout scripture. In Ephesians 2:10, Paul writes, "For we are his workmanship, created in Christ Jesus for good works, which God prepared beforehand, that we should walk in them." This verse affirms that we are not accidents, but masterpieces of God, created with a purpose that was preordained before we even took our first breath. Your purpose is not something that you create; it's something that was given to you by God before the foundations of the world.

As you begin to search for your why, ask yourself: What has God designed me for? What good works has He prepared for me to walk in? To find your why, you must understand that it is already embedded in who you are — your gifts, your desires, your struggles, and your journey.

Looking Through the Lens of God's Design

Once you recognize that you are intentionally designed, it's important to look at your why through the lens of God's greater purpose for your life. Everything in your life, even the brokenness and pain, can be seen through the lens of design. Nothing is wasted in God's kingdom, but that does not mean God allowed the abuse to happen.

Let me share an example from my own life to help explain this process of discovering your why.

When I first found out I was pregnant, my initial why was driven by the desire to give my child a better life than the one I had experienced. My why in that moment was noble: I didn't want my child to go through the pain I had. But as I began to dig deeper, I realized that this was just a starting point — a stepping stone toward something much greater.

I knew, even at that young age, that I didn't want my child to grow up without a father. That was my driving motivation — to provide something that I didn't have. However, as good and as noble as that desire was, it didn't fully align with God's design for family. Back then, I didn't understand what a godly father was or how the relationship between a father and a mother reflected God's design.

Now, looking back, I see how God used that initial why as a launching pad for understanding His divine design. My desire for my son to have a father was rooted in a much deeper need for him to experience God's full intention for family — a healthy, godly father who would lead him, love him, and show him the heart of the Father. The relationship between a father and child is meant to reflect the relationship between God the Father and His children.

In Ephesians 6:4, Paul commands fathers, "Fathers, do not provoke your children to anger, but bring them up in the discipline and instruction of the Lord." This is the design God has for fathers — not to just be present, but to actively guide, nurture, and teach their children about God's love. The role of a father isn't just to show up, but to represent God's heart as a loving, guiding leader in the home.

The Process of Discovery: Investigating Your Why

When you investigate your why, it's crucial to go through a process that helps you look at your motivations, desires, and experiences through the lens of God's design and purpose. Here's how you can do that:

1. Examine the Heart Behind Your Why: Ask yourself why you feel called to do what you're doing. Is it driven by a desire to fulfill your own needs, or is it aligned with God's design for your life and others? For me, my initial why was a desire to protect my child, but as I sought God, I realized that His design for me as a mother and for my child was far bigger. It involved not just providing a safe space but also reflecting God's love, grace, and authority as a parent.

2. Look at Your Desires in Light of God's Word: The desires and passions you have are clues to God's purpose for your life. Psalm 37:4 says, "Delight yourself in the Lord, and he will give you the desires of your heart." This doesn't mean that God will give you anything you want, but that as you align your heart with His, your desires will begin to reflect

His will for you. What are the desires that stir in your heart? Anything can be connected to God's Kingdom purposes. Maybe you love coffee. I am sitting in a coffee shop that is not a "Christian advertisement"; it's actually on a website for a historical haunted property. Ghost Hunters come here. But guess what else is on this property? It's my Church. They have no signage indicating they are a church, but they serve the community by providing a place to work and drink coffee daily. They took their passions for business and coffee and made a place for others to safely dwell in the presence of God, without flaunting it. That is the purpose. That is why. It can be anything. God knit us all together so uniquely. So don't put your why in a box; some of you may go into ministry with your unique testimony, but anything we do can be legacy and ministry.

3. Understand the Bigger Picture: Your why is not just about your personal fulfillment, but about how your life fits into God's grand design. Your purpose is connected to the lives of others and to the furthering of God's Kingdom. What impact do you want to make in the world? How does your why tie into the transformation that God is working in you and through you? And if you can't answer that right now, that's ok. Again, my why started with getting healthy and free to be a good mom.

4. Seek God's Revelation: Ultimately, your why is something that God will reveal to you. As you seek Him through prayer, reading His Word, and being open to His guidance, He will help you understand the deeper purpose behind your life. James 1:5 reminds us, "If any of you lacks wisdom, let him ask of God, who gives to all liberally and without reproach, and it will be given to him." God desires to reveal

His purpose to you, and He will do so when you seek Him earnestly.

You Are the Why: Seeing Yourself Through God's Eyes

As you search for your why, I want you to pause and recognize something powerful:

You are the why.

Before you ever discover a purpose, a calling, or a direction, God Himself chose *you*. He loved you first. He sent His Son for *you*. He wants you whole, healed, restored, and walking in the fullness of who He created you to be. Your why isn't something far away or hidden — it begins with the truth that **your life matters to God.**

Living Out Your Why in the Context of God's Design

When you begin to understand your why through the lens of God's love, everything shifts. Your purpose isn't just about what you do — it's about who you are and who made you. God designed you with intention. He placed gifts, desires, and unique strengths inside you because He has a purpose that only you can fulfill.

For some people, their why becomes clearer as they step into roles like parenthood, marriage, leadership, or service. But even then, the deeper truth remains:

Your why flows out of being loved by God, chosen by God, and created on purpose.

And just as my why unfolded as I grew into the areas God called me to — family, marriage, motherhood — your why is unfolding too. God is gently revealing it as you grow, heal, and open your heart to His design.

Let God Redefine "Normal" for You

As you walk this journey of discovering your why, a huge part of it is learning to see what is truly normal in God's Kingdom. Many of us grew up believing certain behaviors, reactions, and patterns were normal because that's all we saw. Sometimes trauma shaped what we thought was acceptable. Sometimes our environment did. Sometimes, survival mode did.

But God wants to open your eyes to **His** normal—peace, wholeness, truth, love, stability, healing, and identity rooted in Him—because just because something felt familiar in your past doesn't mean it was God's best for you; your why becomes clearer as you let God realign your definition of normal, leading you into a life that reflects His promises, not your past.

The word "normal" is typically defined as something that conforms to a standard, typical pattern, or expected behavior. In general, society dictates what is considered normal, often based on what the majority of people experience or believe. However, from a biblical perspective, normal is not simply what the world has deemed to be common or acceptable—it's what aligns with God's perfect will for our lives.

Romans 12:2 speaks directly to this, saying, "Do not be conformed to this world, but be transformed by the renewal of your mind, that by testing you may discern what the will of God is, what is good and acceptable and perfect." In other words, we are called to break free from the patterns of the world and redefine normal through the lens of God's truth and promises.

Breaking Free from "Normal" Defined by Trauma

Our experiences growing up, especially those marked by trauma, often shape what we perceive to be normal. If we grew up in environments where dysfunction, abuse, neglect, or unhealthy relationships were present, we may have normalized those behaviors and patterns. This isn't to say that these experiences weren't real or painful, but it does mean that they are not what God designed for us to live in.

Trauma often distorts our understanding of what's healthy and what's not. We might believe that chaos, pain, or feeling unworthy is the "normal" way of life because that was all we knew. But God's Word tells us that it is normal for His children to reflect His perfect peace, His love, and His order.

In 2 Corinthians 5:17, the Bible says, "Therefore, if anyone is in Christ, he is a new creation. The old has passed away; behold, the new has come." This verse is powerful because it tells us that even if the pain and dysfunction of our past were "normal," we are not bound to them. Through Christ, we are made new, and God's design for our lives is one of restoration, healing, and transformation.

Let's Gently Check Your Why Against God's Promises

When you're on a healing journey, your why becomes one of the most powerful tools God uses to shape your life. But here's something I learned the hard (and healing) way:

Sometimes our why is still tied to old wounds, fears, or survival patterns, and that's okay—it just means you're human and you've lived through real things. But God loves you too much to let you stay rooted in fear or pain when He has promises full of healing, peace, joy, and freedom for you. So as you think about your why—why you show up, why you push, why you fight, why you love, why you protect, why you work so hard—try asking yourself:

Is my why aligned with God's heart for me, or is it still shaped by the places He wants to heal? No shame. No pressure. Just gentle honesty and invitation. Here are some of God's promises you can use like a heart-check, a compass, a gentle guide back to truth:

1. God's Promise of Healing

"He heals the brokenhearted and binds up their wounds." — Psalm 147:3

Maybe your why has been: *"I don't ever want to get hurt again."*
I get it — I've been there.
But God's desire isn't for you to live guarded or closed off.
His desire is healing — real, deep, soul-level healing.
If your why is built around pain, He's inviting you to rebuild it around **wholeness** instead.

2. God's Promise of Peace

"My peace I give to you... Let not your hearts be troubled." — John 14:27

If your why is something like:
"I have to hold everything together, or everything will fall apart,"
That's not peace — that's pressure.
God's promise for you is peace that doesn't make sense on paper but makes perfect sense in His presence.
If your why feels heavy or anxious, He wants to lighten that

load.

3. God's Promise of Provision

"My God will supply every need of yours..." — Philippians 4:19
When your why is rooted in fear of lack —
"If I don't grind nonstop, we won't make it."
or
"I have to do everything myself,"
— You're carrying something God never asked you to carry alone.
He promises to provide for your needs — financially, emotionally, spiritually, and relationally.
You don't have to live in survival mode anymore.

4. God's Promise of Joy

"The joy of the Lord is your strength." — Nehemiah 8:10
If your why sounds like:
"I don't want to disappoint anyone,"
or
"I have to prove myself,"
That's not joy — that's striving.
God's joy empowers you, strengthens you, and carries you.
Real, God-filled joy takes the pressure off and puts grace back on.

5. God's Promise of a Future and a Hope

**"I know the plans I have for you... plans for hope and a future."
— Jeremiah 29:11**
If your why is connected to fear of the future
or shame about the past,
It's time to let God rewrite that script.
Your future doesn't look like your past —
not when God is the One leading you.

6. God's Promise of Freedom

"If the Son sets you free, you will be free indeed." — John 8:36
If your why still echoes old lies —
"I'm not enough,"
"I'm too broken,"
"I deserve this,"
"I can't change" —
Those are chains Jesus already broke.

God's heart for you is **complete freedom**—freedom in your identity, your choices, your thoughts, your relationships, your purpose. You don't have to live tied to old mindsets anymore.

Let's talk about the enemy's tactics—and why they don't get the final say. One thing I had to learn on my own healing journey is this: when our why isn't rooted in God's truth, the enemy will absolutely try to slip in and influence the places where we're unsure, wounded, or still growing. Not because you're weak. Not because you're failing. But because you're valuable—and he knows it.

Jesus said in John 10:10,

"The thief comes only to steal and kill and destroy, but I

came that they may have life, and have it abundantly." That verse used to scare me, until I realized something powerful: **the enemy attacks what God has anointed. And if he's fighting you, it's because there's something inside you he's terrified of.** He would love to keep you stuck in old patterns, to convince you that trauma is your identity, to plant fear where God is trying to grow freedom. But Jesus didn't come so you would barely survive—He came so you would **thrive, to live abundantly, to** walk in healing, peace, joy, clarity, purpose, and freedom.

So if you're discovering your why and it feels off, or heavy, or rooted in fear, that doesn't mean you're doing something wrong. It simply means God is inviting you into something deeper.

How to Check Your Why With God's Heart

This is something I do often, and I encourage you to try it too:

- Does my why bring peace or pressure?
- Does it line up with Scripture or with fear?
- Does it make me feel small, or does it match how God sees me?
- Does it lead toward healing or back into old cycles?

If something feels misaligned, don't panic. Just ask God, "Lord, show me where I've believed a lie and help me realign with Your truth." He will. He always does. Because he wants you free even more than you want it for yourself. This is a process— sometimes slow, always sacred. And you're not doing it alone.

Why Defining Your Why Is So Powerful for Your Mind, Soul, and Identity

Your why isn't just motivation—it's part of your healing. It's one of the ways God rewrites your story from the inside out. When you start understanding your why, something shifts in your soul:

- Your **mind** begins to think differently.
- Your **emotions** begin to stabilize and heal.
- Your **identity** starts aligning with God's truth instead of past pain.

This is what the Holy Spirit does — He gently transforms us, layer by layer, lie by lie, wound by wound, until we start living as the person God always designed us to be.

You're not trying to become someone new; you're uncovering who you already are in Christ. And that journey—discovering your why, healing with God, stepping into your purpose—is one of the most beautiful things you will ever walk through. I know this from my own story: as I surrendered my pain and let God reveal my true identity, everything began to shift. My testimony is proof that when you let God shape your why, He will do more than just heal your past—He will write a new story of hope and purpose that becomes a testimony to others, too.

Let's Talk About "Normal" — And Why It Doesn't Always Equal God's Best

I want to share something from my own healing journey — something that changed everything for me.

For a long time, I thought certain things were just "normal." The way I felt, the way people treated each other, the chaos I grew up in, or the pain I learned to push down... it all felt normal simply because it was all I knew.

But here's what I learned, and what I want you to hold onto:

Normal does not always mean healthy. Normal does not always mean holy. And normal does not always mean it came from God.

"Normal" just means something became familiar or expected — not that it was God's design for you.

So if you grew up around dysfunction, chaos, fear, criticism, or emotional survival-mode... of course it felt normal. But God's heart for you is so much better than that. His vision for family, relationships, identity, and wholeness is full of peace and blessing. Scripture reminds us in Ephesians 6:1–4 that God's blueprint for the family is built on honor, love, and life-giving connection — not pain.

And if your past didn't look like that, please hear me: you're not broken—you're becoming. I've walked through this, too; my story is living proof that brokenness is not the end but the beginning of becoming who God made you to be. **Now is the perfect time to let God show you what "normal" looks like in His Kingdom, just as He did for me.**

Why Defining Your Why Matters for Your Soul

Your why is not just a cute phrase or a motivational idea—it shapes your whole inner world. When you start discovering your why, your soul (your thoughts, your emotions, your decisions) finally has a direction—a God-direction. I know this personally, because as I began to uncover my own why, I watched God realign every part of my inner world, bringing clarity and hope where there was once confusion. And the Bible tells us exactly how this transformation happens:

"Be transformed by the renewing of your mind..." — Romans 12:2

That word "transformed" means a deep inner change — the kind you feel in your identity, habits, confidence, and healing. God doesn't want you stuck in old cycles. He wants to renew everything within you so you can live out the beautiful purpose He's already spoken over your life.

Vision. Purpose. Identity. (This Is Where It All Gets Real.)

As I grew in my healing journey, I started realizing how connected these things are:

Vision — chazon (חָזוֹן)

This is God showing you where He's taking you. When you start seeing yourself through God's eyes, hope rises again.

"Where there is no vision, the people perish..." — Proverbs 29:18

Purpose — prothesis (πρόθεσις)

This means God has a plan for you, not by accident.

"We are God's handiwork..." — Ephesians 2:10

You were created on purpose **for** a purpose already prepared for you.

Identity — nephesh (נֶפֶשׁ)

This is the core of who you are—your soul, your essence. And God says you are a new creation in Christ (2 Corinthians 5:17). Your identity is not your past, not your trauma, and not your mistakes. Your identity is who God says you are—loved, chosen, restored, whole.

Salvation Is More Than Eternity — It's Healing for Today

One of the most freeing things I learned is that salvation (soteria) isn't just about heaven—it's about your life right now. It's about deliverance, healing, restoration, and freedom in the deepest parts of you. Jesus *wants* to heal the parts of your soul that were wounded by what you thought was "normal."

"By His wounds we are healed..." — Isaiah 53:5

He heals the places that no one sees.

He touches the memories we hide.

He renews what you thought could never be restored.

Here's the Beautiful Truth

Your why matters because **you** matter. And when your why is rooted in God's truth—not fear, not trauma, not survival—your whole life begins to shift. You start stepping out of old patterns and into God's design for you:

freedom, clarity, confidence, healing, purpose, identity, and peace

This is the journey you're on. And I want you to know I'm cheering you on, truly. You are not behind. You are not too late. God is doing something new in you right now.

Take a moment and gently ask yourself:

Does the why I'm living align with God's promises for me?

Does it match who He says I am?

If not, that's okay — this is where the healing begins.

2

Chapter 2: Dreaming Beyond the Wounds

There comes a moment in every healing journey when your *why* opens the door to something even more beautiful: **vision**—the ability to dream again, to imagine the life God always had in mind for you, to see beyond the wounds that once defined you.

I want to begin this chapter by sharing something tender, honest, and true:

My first dream was tiny. It wasn't fancy. It wasn't impressive. It wasn't even spiritual.

Thirteen years ago, when I discovered my real why, my dream was simply *to be a good mom...* and to have a father in my child's life. That was it. That was the biggest thing I could imagine. After everything I had walked through, the idea of stability felt like a miracle all by itself.

Back then, dreaming for me looked like:

— no more panic attacks

— no more depression

— some sense of stability

— beginning to live healthy in my mind, body, spirit, and soul

I even had some material dreams—and God did meet many of them. But what He did over the last 15 years has been far greater than anything I could have bought, decorated, or checked off a list.

In my wildly unexpected journey of finding Christ, I discovered that **His peace** was the real dream.

Contentment — whether I had plenty or very little — became the treasure.

Silencing the enemy's lie that materialism was my worth (a lie rooted in past abuse) became freedom.

And learning to rest in God's presence became the life I didn't even know how to imagine back then.

Learning to Dream Again

In this chapter, I invite you to pause, reflect, and participate.

We're going to take a moment to dream together—actively inviting you to join in the process and imagine what healing could look like in your own life.

I know this might feel strange, especially for those of us with serious lives who grew up quickly in survival mode. We were caretakers and responsible, carrying burdens too heavy for our little hearts. Dreaming didn't feel safe. Imagination seemed foolish. Hope appeared dangerous.

Let me say this with so much love:

For the next few minutes, I want you to let go of that identity.

You can pick it back up later if you want... but I have a feeling you won't need it anymore.

Turn on your favorite song. Take a deep breath. Let your shoulders drop. Let your jaw relax. Let your heart open just a little. Let the little girl inside you come forward. She never got the chance to dream.

A Vision Board: Dreaming With God

Now, don't worry—I made this part *super easy* and actually a lot of fun.

Think of this as a tiny art project between sisters.

In your workbook, if you bought the ARISE Workbook, you'll find some cute templates you can download. Use them. Play with them. Scribble in the margins if you want. Let this be creative, lighthearted, and free. If you didn't buy the workbook, that's OK! You have creative freedom here to do whatever your heart desires.

The first few prompts will guide you into imagining something many of us didn't even know how to picture at first:

"What would a day of complete healing look like for me?"

If your immediate answer is "I have no idea," you're in good company. I felt the exact same way for years. I couldn't imagine peace, joy, or freedom. I couldn't imagine waking up without dread. I couldn't imagine relationships without triggers. I couldn't imagine life without a constant, internal war. But today, I can tell you what my healing looks like. Not perfectly, but beautifully. I live without panic attacks, depression, or constant hyper-vigilance.

I once had panic attacks every day. I stayed in my room for months because I felt safer. Nightmares, PTSD, unwanted memories, and confusing emotions haunted me.

I felt like the "odd one out" for choosing health. I felt alone, unheard, and exhausted. But then God healed me, layer by layer, day by day, in ways no pill ever could. Today I laugh—real, belly-deep laughter I didn't even know I was capable of. I have joy. I have safe, loving, beautiful women in my life who feel like family. I know how to keep my love on through healthy boundaries. I met the little girl inside me, once terrified and alone. And now? I feel safe. Truly safe. I live in peace, not panic. I respond instead of react. I have learned, for the most part, when to speak and when to stay silent. Trials still come—they always will. My husband and I both lost a parent in the same seven months. Grief came. Memories resurfaced. Triggers were offered. But the difference was this: I stayed grounded. I stayed safe. I stayed in peace. That's what a healed vision looks like for me now. And it's what I believe is possible for you, too.

Sister, I believe in you. I also know that sometimes it can feel almost impossible to believe healing is meant for you. If you have doubts or wonder if this promise could really include you, please know you are not alone. Doubt is simply part of being human, especially after walking through so much pain. If your heart feels hesitant or afraid to hope, I gently encourage you to bring those feelings honestly to God—He can handle them all. Let me offer a simple prayer for you: Jesus, meet my sister here in her doubts. Hold her close and remind her that healing is possible, even when she struggles to see it. Renew her hope day by day.

As you create your vision board, hear this with every fiber of your being: Trauma is not stronger than the blood of Jesus. (As I've emphasized throughout this chapter, what He did in me, He can absolutely do in you.) This healing journey was never meant to be exclusive. God doesn't heal favorites—He heals daughters who come close. I have laid my life down to walk beside you as you discover yours.

So dream big, my sister. Dream boldly. Dream with God. Dream with your healed future in mind. Big dreams are coming for you—bigger than you've even dared to imagine.

Imagination: The Womb of Your Future

Before we move on, I want to introduce something beautiful. It's ancient, biblical, and deeply connected to what you're about to step into. In Hebrew thought, the word for imagination connects to formation, shaping, and birthing. It paints the picture of a womb. This is a hidden place. Here, something unseen is knit together by God before it is revealed.

Your imagination is not childish. It is sacred. It is the spiritual womb where God plants vision. When you dream, when you imagine a life healed and whole, you are allowing God to place something in the womb of your spirit—something growing, something forming, something preparing to be birthed.

That's where we are now. You've found your why. You're dreaming again. Now, like a womb ready for birth, we'll move through the nine phases that bridge your why to your dream. Each phase is a gentle step, guiding you from intention to new reality. In these next pages, I'll walk you through all nine—so you'll never feel lost or overwhelmed along the way. Get ready to explore the path from uncovering your purpose, to creating safe space, to embracing community, and all the way to living out your healed vision each day. Up first is Phase One, a foundation that will give you solid ground as you step forward. Let's see what it looks like together.

A Little Birthing Pep Talk

You know I have five children now. It has been a long time since those early days of my healing journey, and each of those babies came naturally. Spoiler alert: that boyfriend I got pregnant from is now my husband, and together we are creating this legacy. With each of our births, I started speaking something out loud:

"I am not going into labor, I am going into favor," I said

it every time. I corrected nurses, doctors, and myself. Why? Scripture says it's not by works but by His favor. The word "works" in the original language is linked to child labor—painful striving and pushing.

God never asked you to heal by striving. He never asked you to push until you break or to work your way into freedom. Healing is not labor. Healing flows from favor.

As a baby grows in the womb without force, your healing grows by grace, presence, alignment, openness, breath, and trust. Let God do the forming. You're not entering labor—you're entering favor.

What Comes Next

Now that you have found your why, awakened your imagination, and allowed God to plant vision in the womb of your spirit, we get to walk step by step through the nine phases that build the bridge from where you are to where God is taking you.

(As mentioned earlier in the imagination section,) this is where your dream becomes a process—a formation, a journey, a birthing, a becoming.

And I promise you, you will not do it alone. I am with you. The Holy Spirit is with you. Your sisters in this journey are with you. The trauma is not stronger than the blood of Jesus. And what God has birthed in me, He is ready to birth in you. If you are longing for connection along the way, consider seeking out a few places where you can journey together:

You might join our online group where we journey through the 10 weeks together, side by side. More info in the back of the book and the front! If you feel led, invite a friend to become a prayer partner and commit to praying for each other's healing.

Or look for gatherings in your local church or community, where you can share, listen, and grow together face to face. If you don't know where to start, reach out to your church or message me, and I can help you find resources or groups to connect with. You are never meant to heal in isolation—there are sisters waiting to come alongside you.

Prepare yourself. Your dream is not only possible; it's already forming.

Let's step into Phase One together.

3

Chapter 3:The Question Every Survivor Asks

Before we dive into this next phase, let us pause together and welcome the Holy Spirit.

I want this to become a rhythm for you, a holy habit. Take a moment, breathe, and invite Him into this chapter, this lesson, and this part of your healing journey.

If you have access to a worship song, go ahead and play it. If not, or if you prefer not to, you can simply sing a song of praise in your heart, or open with words of thanksgiving. Worship is a weapon. When we worship, our hearts soften, our minds open, and His presence fills the space where fear, confusion, and heaviness once lived.

As the worship plays or your heart sings, feel free to talk with God or simply sit with Him. Ask the Holy Spirit to come close. He loves being invited. If you are new to knowing the Holy Spirit, or this whole relationship feels unfamiliar, that is okay. Be sure to listen to the teaching on the Holy Spirit later, but for now, just know this.

He is here. He is alive. And He is Jesus' gift to you. He is your Teacher, your Helper, your Guide, your Comforter, your Counselor. He is the safest friend you will ever have. So go ahead and **invite Him on this journey with you**. He is ready to walk every step with you.

Now, let me share how understanding His presence became real to me through my own healing story.

Wow. Do you feel that? Worship has a way of touching places in us we didn't even know needed healing. Deliverance happens in His presence. Peace rises. Walls fall.

With that in mind, since we just worshiped together, let's transition to talking honestly about His presence for a moment.

When I first started my healing journey, I didn't really understand God at all. I knew I needed Jesus. I knew something inside me was crying out for Him. But I didn't know His character. I didn't know His heart. I didn't know who He really was.

To be honest, I had the completely wrong picture of Him.

I saw God as a skywatcher, constantly monitoring my mistakes and waiting to punish me. I thought following Him meant strict obedience, and I confused fear with the "fear of the Lord." It was religion, not trust, that almost prevented my healing.

How could I trust someone with the title "Father," when my earthly father abused me, wounded me, and abandoned me? How could I run to God when I believed He had allowed everything horrible that happened in my life?

How could I open my heart when I thought He was the one who wanted me to tough it out, suffer, and "learn a lesson"? I truly believed God caused the trauma so I would be stronger for Him later.

I truly believed He looked at my childhood and said, "This will teach her something." All of that was wrong. It came from religion and pain, not truth. What changed my life in an instant was this realization: **God is good.** Not "good except when..." Not "good unless..." Not "good but mysterious in a scary way..." No. **God is good, and there is no darkness in Him at all.**

For me, everything shifted when I heard the lyrics of a worship song that said:

"There is nothing I have to do but be with You.

It's You and me, and me and You.

We are returning to the desire of Your heart."

That line broke something open in me. Because I finally realized something I had never been taught: God's desire has always been closeness. Friendship. Union. Fatherhood. Just like in the Garden before sin came in and distorted our view of Him. God's heart was never for trauma. God's heart was never for abandonment. God's heart was never for your suffering. His desire—from the very beginning—was for you to know His goodness and experience His love without fear. God is good. And when that truth finally sank into my bones, it became the foundation of my healing. Believing God is good changes everything. This is the cornerstone. When you believe God is not good, or that he is in conflict with his own word, or that he sent calamity or disease or tragedy, then that belief becomes the cornerstone of all your theology. It is in believing he is good that our hearts are restored to stability. I grew up without much stability, and it feels so good to be restored.

God is good is more than a positive thought, a theological concept, or a biblical statement. What you do with these three worlds defines your reality and determines your destiny. "Bill Johnson" When we know God is good, we know everything will turn out for his glory, and we also know his presence is in every moment. It allows us to take a different stance. Instead of asking God why something is happening, why he allowed it, or where he is, we position ourselves in communion with the Father and become part of the solution.

After I accepted Jesus into my heart, I believed bad theology for four years, over half of my Christian life at that point. I believed that God was allowing things like cancer, depression, and anxiety to happen to me. I believed he was doing this to make me closer to him. I did not understand his character at all, but I knew deep down it felt scary and wrong. A lot of this came from not having a trustworthy biological father and having a stepfather who meant well but was very militant and strict. I was left in a space between fear and striving. Little by little, I started to have a stirring in my spirit that God was good, but I still held back.

I would pray for giant things like healing from cancer, and I would see him move. But he would also move in tiny little details of my life and fulfill desires in my heart. That became the foundation of an intimate father-daughter relationship. Forgiveness played a huge role in helping me understand his character. One very specific morning, he became present and alive to me. I met my sponsor for Step Studies at the bay early in the morning. A couple of months earlier, I heard a message about seeing porpoises in the bay. I thought there was no way, but how amazing would that be? I wanted to see porpoises so bad because, you know, I love all things beach. That morning, while sharing my inventory, I went through a list of events and people who had hurt me, sharing my reactions and my parts in each situation. When we held hands to pray, my hands were shaking, my voice was stuttering, and my stomach hurt. But when we said Amen, I looked up, and there was a huge pod of porpoises moving through the bay. This intimate moment was one of the small moments between Abba and me that began to cultivate the relationship we have to this day.

After forgiving my biological father, I was able to release all resistance and finally trust Abba with my healing. I trusted that his character was good. I was able to look through the lens of God is good and step into hope, while striving and confusion fell to the ground.

With that foundation, let's now explore how this understanding connects with the story of Jesus Himself.

Jesus Christ is the perfect theology and one rad brother. In the Old and New Testaments, there are times when they seem to be in conflict, and there is no denying that. Jesus comes on the scene and resolves the issues of the Old Testament in the New Testament. I am not saying the Old Testament is wrong. Its purpose and message were different.

The Old Testament was written to reveal the severity of sin. It was written to create an awareness of the need for a Savior and to point to Jesus as that Savior. When Jesus arrives, he shows us more clearly the heart of the Father. Hebrews 1 says he is the exact representation of the Father's nature. He became the exact manifestation of the Father. When you see him healing people, that is the Father's heart. When you see him not stoning the woman caught in adultery, that is the Father's heart. You see a father-daughter moment. You see a Father embracing a lost, wounded daughter and showing her through love who she really is. Just like the woman at the well.

I can relate to both of these women. God did not confront me in wrath for the life I used to live. I was involved in drugs, alcohol, partying, sex, and using men for relationships. I lied, hurt people, stole, and made many bad choices. Then the love of Jesus hit me, and people no longer recognized me. I was healed, delivered, and set free through the heart of the Father and the blood of Jesus Christ.

I want you to know, friend, if Jesus could do that for me, he can do it for you, too. No matter what pain, shame, or trauma has defined your past, Jesus can heal. He can restore. He can redeem.

We would never let the Old Testament animal sacrifices substitute for the sacrifice of Jesus and his blood, yet the church sometimes lowers its standard regarding disease, conflict, calamity, and death. Sometimes it even surpasses the example Jesus set. That is not how God operates. I cannot explain it all fully, but I can embrace the example Jesus gave. And that example has transformed my life. It has freed me from the effects of sexual abuse, trauma, and fear.

Jesus slept at the bottom of the boat in the middle of a life-threatening storm. He slept because the world he lived in had no storms. He released peace over the storm because he carried peace within him. We know he had peace because he slept in the storm. And I want to encourage you: you can have that peace too. The storms may come, but he gives you strength and calm in the midst of them. Can God give away sickness? No, because he does not have a sickness to give away. Does God ever choose not to heal? No. Two thousand years ago, he made the ultimate purchase through Jesus. Just like when you buy a car in cash, you cannot go back and decide not to buy it. The purchase has been made. God's payment through Jesus was sufficient for all sin or no sin, all sickness or no sickness. Healing and forgiveness work together because they were the two main things Jesus' stripes and blood addressed. There is also one more: poverty. In Matthew, when it says deliver us from evil, the word comes from the word pain. Pain comes from the root word poor. God's redemption was designed to wipe out the root of sin, illness, and poverty.

What about Paul's thorn? I do not believe it was sickness. Paul referred to his eye, but the Bible is written in an ancient, mostly Eastern context, not a Western cultural mindset. Paul knew the Old Testament very well. There are only two references in the Old Testament to a thorn in the flesh, and neither of them was about sickness. I want to encourage you: the struggles you face are not the final word. You can walk in freedom, healing, and hope. I know what it is like to feel broken, unseen, and wounded. I know what it is like to carry shame and fear. But I also know what it is like to experience the Father's love in such a real, tangible way that your life is transformed. That is what I am walking in today, and it is what is waiting for you, too. Your story is not over. Your healing is coming. You are not defined by the storm, the abuse, or the pain. You are defined by Jesus Christ, the perfect example of love, grace, and redemption.

His Word says:"10 The thief comes only to steal and kill and destroy; he has come that you may have life, and have it to the full." John 10:10

The thief is the enemy, little Lucy, aka the devil. What happened to you fits squarely into little Lucy's job description, not God's. He came to steal, kill, and destroy your life. I know exactly how that feels because I lived it too. Sexual abuse and trauma steal so much—safety, security, confidence, your body, your mind, your relationships. The list goes on and on. But God has come so you may have life and have it to the full. It is true. I am living it right now.

One of my favorite promises to live by is from Proverbs 19:23:

"When you live a life of abandoned love, surrendered before the awe of God, here's what you'll experience: abundant life, continual protection, and complete satisfaction."

Friends, abundant life, continual protection, and complete satisfaction. This is everything you have dreamed of and more. Amen. Continual protection—when I used to be triggered, it was always because I felt unsafe. There is nothing better than continual protection from the Creator of the universe.

So what does it mean to live a life of abandoned love, surrendered before the awe of God? Some translations of the Bible call this the fear of God. I want to tell you that the fear of God is literally just being so in love with Him and His kindness that you never want to be out of His presence. It is a heart that constantly seeks Him, knowing He is kind and good, and believing in His promises.

And now for the question I hear the most: Did he allow it? You might be thinking, " Living an abundant life with continual protection and complete satisfaction sounds amazing. But where was His protection when the abuse happened? Did He allow it so that one day you could help others or grow closer to Him?

The answer is no. He did not allow it. God is an amazing Father. He is not like our earthly parents or our abusers. He is good all the time. He does not allow crisis and tragedy for a purpose. He put us in a realm where our authority and will affect what happens around us. That does not mean we carry guilt or shame for tragedy, but it does mean we take ownership of the life we are given. Think about Jesus. How many storms did He bless? None. Jesus did not send storms to harm a city or to humble people and bring them closer to God. That would not represent the Father. Hebrews 1 describes Jesus as the exact representation of the Father.

Believing that everything that comes our way is God's will makes it hard to trust Him to change things. He is not an egomaniac. There is a difference between being in charge and being in control. If you think He is in control of everything, then you might also think that Hitler was acting under God's will and that God was powerless to stop it. That is not the God of the Bible. God comes at our invitation because He has given us dominion over this earth. God can step onto the stage anytime He wants, but C.S. Lewis put it best: when the Author steps onto the stage, the play is over. Are we ready for the play to be over? Not yet. There are still many lost sisters and brothers living in darkness, and He has called us to shine His light until the end.

Part of living and abiding in the realm of faith that God is good is representing God's goodness wherever we go. Being filled with the Father's love and revelation is a gift that keeps giving. That is why we are not yet ready for the Author to walk on the stage and end it all. We know we will be with Him for eternity. Now, we get to share the goodness of the Father with others. Generosity is not just about money; it is about showing compassion, love, and hope. It is encouraging and building up. It is speaking life-giving words from our heart to our tongue. Friends, I want you to remember this: the enemy may have stolen from you, but he cannot take the abundant life that Jesus paid for. You are meant to live in continual protection and complete satisfaction. You are meant to represent the Father's goodness in a world that desperately needs it.

If God didn't orchestrate the storm, then why did it happen? Well, who did He leave in charge? Who did He disciple, who did He teach when He said, "As the Father sent me, I send you"?

I have five kids, and it was after having them that I really began to understand the love of God as a parent. He is a loving, protective Father and gentle like a mother.

I would never let you babysit my children and allow you to

abuse them. No way. But if you did abuse them when I wasn't there, that would be completely out of my control and a product of your own will. People who abuse children or adults are out of the presence of God and operating in their own free will, which is not of God. Even if someone who says they believe was your abuser, their life proved otherwise. The Bible says you will know them by their fruit.

My friend once gave me an analogy that helped me understand this. We were born into a battle. Ephesians 6:12 speaks on this:

"Your hand-to-hand combat is not with human beings, but with the highest principalities and authorities operating in rebellion under the heavenly realms. They are a powerful class of demon-gods and evil spirits that hold this dark world in bondage."

The only thing God allowed was for us to have free will, so when we choose Him, we do so by surrendering our own will to be part of His. His will is abundant life. Little Lucy's will is to steal, kill, and destroy. And we get to choose as His creation what our will is going to be.

I'm guessing many of you are very strong-willed. It has taken a lot of strength to reach this point in your journey. Some of you will have to intentionally surrender. But Jesus said in the Bible, "Not my will, but Your will be done." This means you can have a will to do something and, at the same time, surrender to His will.

Here's a simple example, and it might seem silly, but it taught me a lot. Last night, as I was writing this course in a beautiful vacation home that was donated to support all of you on your healing journey, I accidentally left the cap off my new, passionately pink marker. The ink soaked through a quilt, two sheets, a mattress pad, and onto the mattress. Yikes! My first thought was, "Oh man, this sucks. Maybe I should flip the quilt over or the mattress?" But then God's will spoke to me. "No problem. I promise to provide for all your needs. Show love and my good character. Order new bedding, have it shipped tomorrow, and show your hosts a lifestyle of Christianity. They know why you are here."

It's so simple, right?

The Bible actually says that meekness doesn't mean weakness. It says meekness means strength under control. Matthew 5:5 promises, "Blessed are the meek, for they will inherit the earth." God is not going to take your strength away. He loves your strength. But if you are strong, as I was, let me tell you: the Holy Spirit will be your best friend, because you will learn to be led. It might feel harder for you than for others, but your outcome will be amazingly epic.

Now, let's go back to my friend's analogy. We were born into a battle. Imagine you are the general of an army going into battle. You are in charge of your troops. You have been training them, encouraging them, giving them battle plans, and helping to renew their minds. You commune with them. You position yourselves close together. You give them dominion and trust them as you send them to war.

Then, someone on the front line decides your battle strategy doesn't work. They bring two others in a different direction because their will and pride led them to think they knew better. This results in all three tripping into a landmine, giving the enemy a direct path to your other troops. Your front three get injured, and your troops are blindsided and left vulnerable. Your troops are hurt, and some are killed. Is this your fault? Did you allow it? No. You were in charge but not in control of what they did with the dominion you entrusted to them.

Knowing you, because you are a good general, you see the three who tripped. The enemy is coming right behind them. You jump in front and take the wrath of the enemy on yourself because you love your troops. That is exactly what God did for us. God came down in human form as Jesus and took the wrath for all sin so we could walk in abundant life, abandoned love, and surrender to the Kingdom of Heaven here on earth, in relationship with the Holy Spirit.

The Holy Spirit's job is to present you in Christ before Abba. His job is to develop who you are in Jesus. He will be the one talking to you the most about Jesus because he adores Him. He will help you with everything you face. Jesus is in heaven praying for you. The Holy Spirit is on earth, living out those prayers in you. You do not have to strive because He will make sure you connect with it here on earth. He is with you every day. The presence of God will never depend on your emotions. His presence will never leave. He is here because He said He would be.

If you are brand new to the concept of the Holy Spirit or even a veteran in your faith, please check out the Holy Spirit resources in your portal.

So friends, as we close this chapter, I want to leave you with the most essential truth: **God did not allow the abuse you experienced.** (As explained above, what was done to you was never His will, plan, or purpose.) The enemy comes to steal, kill, and destroy, but Jesus came so that you may have life, and life abundantly (John 10:10). Your abuse aligns with the enemy's nature—not God's.

Before you move forward, I want to invite you into a moment of stillness. Pause. Breathe. Let your heart settle. Invite the Holy Spirit to speak.

You don't need to imagine what life looks like fully healed right now. You don't have to create a future vision.

Instead, I want you to simply ask: "God, what are You saying to me right now?" This may come as a whisper, a sense, a word, a scripture, a feeling of peace, or even a picture. It will never contradict His truth or character. It will never shame you or blame you. It will always align with His heart revealed in Scripture.

In the Hebrew Scriptures, God's nature has always been clear. Psalm 34:18 says, "The Lord is near to the brokenhearted and saves those who are crushed in spirit." The Hebrew word for "saves" is *yasha* — to deliver, rescue, defend, and restore. God's nature is to rescue you, not to allow harm to come upon you. He is the God who heals the brokenhearted (*rapha shabar* in Hebrew — to mend what has been shattered).

He is the God who binds up wounds (*chabash* — to wrap, comfort, and secure). He is the God who restores years that were stolen (Joel 2:25).

He is the God who carries you in your affliction, not the one who authored it.

And He still wants you healed—even if you never stand on a stage, never share a testimony, never lead a group, and never "use" your healing for anything outward. He wants you healed because **you are His child**, because your heart matters, because your freedom matters, because your life matters.

But when you choose to step into healing and surrender to His leading, something powerful happens. Your life becomes a living witness of His goodness. Not because you strive, or perform, or prove anything, but because His love naturally flows through a healed and surrendered heart.

So as we close this chapter, I want you to pause and genuinely ask God: **"Father, what are You saying to me right now?"** Write what you sense. Journal it. Sit with it. The Holy Spirit is faithful to confirm truth. He is gentle. He is present. He is near. And remember—as emphasized throughout this chapter— your abuse was never God's will. Your healing absolutely is. And He will walk you through every step of it.

4

Chapter 4: The Spiritual Reality: How To Battle

The Spiritual Reality: How Knowing the Battle Changes Everything

Welcome to this chapter, where we explore how understanding the spiritual battle truly transforms our lives.

This chapter will be short and sweet. We are going to cover **what spiritual warfare is** and how to kick Little Lucy's (aka the devil's) booty.

When I was praying over this book, I felt really led to include this chapter—even though it wasn't originally planned. When I was walking through my own healing journey, I had no idea that spiritual warfare even existed. And when I found out about it, I was terrified!

That's why I am so excited to break it down for you.

Spiritual warfare is not as frightening as it seems; in fact, much of the intimidation we feel is an illusion. The enemy often uses fear, accusation, and lies to convince us he has more power than he actually does. What feels overwhelming can often be traced back to deceptive thoughts or emotions that do not hold true authority over us. That being said, the struggles you face are very real and can feel intense—this is not to minimize your experience. The illusion is not the struggle itself, but the idea that you are powerless or that the enemy is stronger than God's protection and your spiritual authority. Let's get clear on the truth, recognize your authority, and step forward in confidence.

Before we dive into this important conversation, let's pause and invite Jesus into this moment with us. He is our power, our protection, and our guide.

Don't you just love worship?

I truly believe worship is a weapon against spiritual warfare, and I also believe that most of spiritual warfare—about ninety percent—is fought through the renewing of your mind, believing in your identity, and walking in it.

Now that we've set the stage with worship, let's answer a foundational question: What is spiritual warfare?

Kris Vallotton from KrisVallotton.com gives one of the best definitions, and I have included a link to his blog in the resources tab in your student portal if you have bought the ARISE COURSE. Kris says:

"Spiritual *conflicts most often occur when we advance into new territory that is inhabited by evil spirits. Much like Joshua's promised land experience or Nehemiah's rebuilding of the walls, the enemy defends his territory when we are pushing forward into the new land. Most Christians are completely unaware that these are real spirit wars, so they retreat at the first sign of conflict, failing to recognize the true source of the battle.*"

It is important to understand that evil spirits attack by prompting you to have compelling thoughts. They make you feel like you want to act on them, even though they are the opposite of your nature and your history. They convince you that you are a victim, unworthy, or that God won't provide for you. Then those same spirits accuse you of having these thoughts and feelings, making you believe it was your fault and that something is wrong with you.

If you believe these accusations, you lose confidence in yourself and in God's ability to protect you, and the shame cycle begins. This can spiral into depression, anxiety, and self-hatred. If I had read this at the start of my journey, I might have quit out of fear, but that's why I want to equip you now. You are here because you're ready to move beyond what's holding you back, and knowing the real battle helps you do that.

So suit up, mighty lioness warrior. You are about to claim your territory, your promised land, and walk in the freedom God has already purchased for you.

Ways to Suit Up

Let's talk about identity. You've probably heard about identity a lot—you are a child of God—but it's one thing to hear it and another to actually walk in it.

Walking in your identity is the most important way to prepare for spiritual warfare. Genesis 1:27 tells us we are made in His image. Did you know Jesus actually calls us His equal? The word sister can be translated as " his equal. In scripture, we are told not to be unequally yoked, and the fact that Abba yoked His Son with us shows we are His equal.

We were crucified with Him and co-raised with Him in resurrection power. We will be His co-heirs for all eternity. Just as [in His love] He chose us in Christ [actually selected us for Himself as His own] before the foundation of the world, so that we would be holy [consecrated, set apart for Him, purpose-driven] and blameless in His sight.

In love, He predestined and lovingly planned for us to be

adopted to Himself as [His own] children through Jesus Christ, in accordance with the kind intention and good pleasure of His will—to the praise of His glorious grace and favor, which He so freely bestowed on us in the Beloved, His Son, Jesus Christ. In Him we have redemption, our deliverance and salvation through His blood, which paid the penalty for our sin and resulted in the forgiveness and complete pardon of our sin, in accordance with the riches of His grace which He lavished on us.

In all wisdom and understanding, He made known to us the mystery of His will according to His good pleasure, which He purposed in Christ, with regard to the fulfillment of the times—to bring all things together in Christ, both things in the heavens and things on the earth. In Him also we have received an inheritance, a destiny—we were claimed by God as His own—having been predestined according to the purpose of Him who works everything in agreement with the counsel and design of His will, so that we who first put our confidence in Christ would exist to the praise of His glory.

In Him, you also, when you heard the word of truth, the good news of your salvation, and believed in Him, were stamped with the seal of the promised Holy Spirit, the One promised by Christ, as owned and protected by God. The Spirit is the guarantee, the first installment, the pledge, a foretaste of our inheritance until the redemption of God's purchased possession, His believers, to the praise of His glory. If you take just one thing from this section, let it be this:

You were chosen before the world began to be God's child. As Jesus's sister in faith, you have full access as a co-heir and carry genuine spiritual authority as Abba's daughter. Pause for a moment and soak this in. Think about it. When we believed in Him, we were stamped with the seal of the promised Holy Spirit as owned and protected by God.

Hold up. Let's really let this sink in.

Jesus died on the cross. He endured the most horrific death and suffering anyone on this earth has ever faced. He fought the most intense spiritual warfare the world has ever seen. He died and was raised from the dead, gifting us our salvation and our access to our inheritance. Stepping into our identity as a child of God, the ultimate trophy of that victory in this phase of history is the Holy Spirit—and we are sealed with Him.

The sealing Paul speaks of refers to an official mark of identification, like a signet on a letter or contract. The seal identified the document as authentic and placed it under the authority of the one who sealed it.

This is exactly what God has done for us. We are officially stamped, owned, and protected by Him. When you walk into that truth, you are fully suited up for spiritual warfare. If spiritual warfare seems daunting, remember—it's actually just a huge mirage.

We are seated at a table in the presence of our enemies. This means we get to position ourselves in the most intimate place with our Abba Daddy, our heavenly Father. We don't focus on the enemies around us, but we dine in intimacy with our Father. He gives us the secret recipe for the meal of victory we are eating, and that recipe is His Word.

Never forget, your identity as His daughter secures your victory. Remember our verse from Proverbs 19:23:

"When you live a life of abandoned love, surrendered before the awe of God, here's what you'll experience: abundant life, continual protection, and complete satisfaction." We are continually protected as we seek and live for Him. Believe it, even with a mustard seed of faith. Let's get practical: worship and rest are powerful weapons.

Anything that comes your way, position yourself in a posture of worship. Realize that not every bad thing that happens is the enemy.

Don't give Little Lucy credit—he doesn't deserve it. For example, if you forget to put gas in your car and it runs out, that is a natural consequence. Or if I decided to eat every time I had a craving for sugar and developed type 2 diabetes, that is also a natural consequence.

Find the root behind the constant cravings. Is it a spirit, as Kris Vallotton talked about? If so, it's time to take charge, renew your mind, and take authority over this voice.

Grab your sword, which comes from the word Rhema, meaning a quick, specific word from God. Remember in Chapter 2 when the Holy Spirit gave me a word and a verse about abundant life to use as my Rhema, my sword? It worked.

Sit with Him and ask Him for a strategy in this battle.

Take a survey of the input you are allowing into your heart and mind. What kind of shows are you watching? Do they align with an abundant life? What kind of songs are you singing?

There are spiritual influences in many of the things we surround ourselves with in this world. I am not saying to give up everything, but to ask the Holy Spirit for sweet conviction if something you are allowing into your life is hurting your heart and mind in the long run. Sometimes this even means adjusting relationships with friends or family. Remember, the Holy Spirit will never shame or guilt you. His conviction is always sweet.

Kris Vallotton shared an amazing way to battle: remember the testimonies in your life; they are weapons of warfare.

Fill yourself with faith by holding onto testimonies from others' lives, too. Revelation 19:10 says, "The testimony of Jesus is the spirit of prophecy."

This means if God has done it before, He can and will do it again.

Let me illustrate with a personal story—a turning point that came with a huge battle.

I was taking Kris Vallotton's course, Spirit Wars. The course was a huge struggle for me. It was intense, vivid, and confronting, and I felt like a little girl terrified of the monster under her bed.

I actually stopped going to the sessions because it was all too much for me. And remember, this was all before I had any of the revelations from Part 1.

Then one morning, I rose up and decided I had enough.

I watched week 7 from home, and it completely changed my life. That was the day I realized I had a gift called atmospheric discernment.

Atmospheric discernment means you can sense the spiritual atmosphere in places or around people. You can feel the tone, the pressure, the influence, or the spiritual authority operating in a room or within someone's life.

I have noticed that many of my clients carry this same gift. I personally believe that when someone has experienced sexual abuse, something in their spirit becomes acutely sensitive to spiritual atmospheres. Not in a broken way, but in a heightened way. It becomes a gift of survival that God later turns into a weapon of discernment.

And in my own journey and in those I've walked with, I rarely see it disappear. Instead, it becomes redeemed, strengthened, and purified as healing takes place.

Before I understood any of this, I would experience extreme reactions in certain environments and had no idea why.

For example, my husband and I visited a mega church in our city several times. Every single time we parked our car and stepped onto that property, out of nowhere, I would start bawling, convinced my husband was cheating on me or about to cheat on me.

These thoughts were irrational and had no basis in reality. They felt like they came from nowhere and left me feeling bipolar, unstable, or crazy. My husband felt the tension too, even though he didn't know why.

Later, we learned that the pastor of that church was involved in multiple sexual scandals. What I had been reacting to was the spiritual atmosphere and the authority influencing that building.

I wasn't crazy. I was discerning. I just didn't know what to call it yet. This type of thing is more common than people realize.

Someone can leave their house in a great mood, then walk into work and suddenly feel depression, anxiety, suspicion, or heaviness.

While not every emotional shift is spiritual, sometimes this is a sign of atmospheric discernment.

If you are someone who feels intense emotions in certain places, or you experience sudden shifts in feelings when you walk into different environments, or you struggle with social anxiety that seems to come out of nowhere, I want to encourage you to explore this area.

It may be a gift, not a flaw. It may be discernment, not instability.

But for right now, the most important thing is this. Walk and talk with the Holy Spirit as these feelings arise. Pause with Him. Ask Him what is yours and what is not. Ask Him what belongs to the atmosphere and what belongs to your own heart. Allow

Him to guide you moment by moment.

You are not alone in this, and you are not crazy. You might simply be gifted.

Maybe you have felt something in your home. Maybe when you leave the house, you feel relief, but when you walk back in, you feel heaviness, depression, or lethargy.

Maybe you can't pinpoint it, but something feels "off" or spiritually thick.

You may be facing something territorial or something that is hovering over the environment. These things do not have authority over you, but they can influence an atmosphere if they are not confronted.

We are going to talk about how to combat these issues, and then we will touch on something many people never understand, but that deeply affects their healing journey: generational curses or patterns. To support you as you read, I want you to know that I will be sharing practical steps you can take— including specific prayers, ways to discern spiritual influences in your life, and simple actions to invite God's protection and freedom into your story. Help is coming. By the end of this chapter, you will have clear guidance and tools to walk in victory.

I want to preface this very clearly.

I never want to give the enemy too much power, and I certainly do not want you to walk in fear.

I also want to acknowledge that I do not know the extent of my biological father's family line. I only know what was revealed from my mom's side and, later, my husband's.

I have lived on both sides of the coin—wisdom and ignorance. There were years when I didn't know or believe generational curses were real. Even in those years of not knowing, it was the grace and mercy of God that kept me alive, sustained my soul, and walked me through some wild seasons.

Grace is God doing a work in the human soul that we cannot do ourselves.

Grace is the power of God moving in our weakness. Grace is protection, intervention, help, and empowerment, even when we don't understand what's happening.

The warfare I went through at the beginning of my healing journey was intense. But here's the wild part: I didn't know it was warfare. I thought it was just me being broken or losing my mind.

I remember seeing things move in our house. I had massive anxiety attacks.

Deep depression. Sleepless nights.

At one point, I was diagnosed with postpartum psychosis. I took one pill, and this is not medical advice, but I immediately knew in my spirit I wasn't meant to continue.

I felt lifeless, numb, disconnected from myself. So I did the only thing I knew to do—I prayed. I prayed and prayed and prayed some more.

During that season, a demon-possessed man would come to our house and taunt us. He would expose himself and threaten to kill my son and me. It sounds unbelievable, but it is exactly what happened.

What is even more shocking is that every house on our street was attacked during that year except ours. Not one time did he touch our home. Not once did he come onto our property. He stood at a distance and screamed, but he never crossed the boundary line. God's protection was hovering over us.

Even though I didn't know much at the time, my husband and I were both seeking the Lord in the way we understood righteousness. God honored that. His mercy covered our ignorance. His grace covered the gaps.

About seven years later, people began coming up to us with words of knowledge about a Freemasonry curse in the family line.

I didn't know what that even meant. But my husband knew immediately. His grandfather was one of the highest-ranking masons on *both* sides of the family. Generationally, that holds a lot of spiritual weight.

But here is what I want to emphasize. God did not reveal that until we were strong enough to handle it. He revealed it at the perfect time, after years of healing and growth, because He is kind.

He doesn't reveal demons to scare us; He reveals them so we can evict them. And by the time this surfaced, I had enough wisdom, authority, and spiritual maturity to face it without fear.

My husband also learned new information that elevated his accountability as the gatekeeper of our generational bloodline.

This season of breakthrough took us to new levels of freedom, but it also brought us to new levels of warfare.

Not because the enemy was big—but because God was revealing, healing, and uprooting things that had been there for generations.

And the same God who did it for me will do it for you.

As you step deeper into your healing journey, I want you to hold a visual metaphor in your heart, something that will help you distinguish between warfare in the mind and real spiritual warfare.

Picture yourself standing in a long, ancient hallway. The walls are stone, cool and worn, and there are doors on both sides. Some of the doors are cracked open, and light pours through them. These are the places where God is inviting you deeper into truth, freedom, identity, and healing.

Then there are other doors—closed, rattling, shadows pushing from underneath. Those doors represent the enemy's attempts to get your attention, to pull you off path, or to convince you that you are still trapped in something you've already been delivered from.

The enemy has no legal access to you anymore. Those doors are locked from your side, not his. The only way he gains ground is if you stop walking, stand in the hallway, and start focusing on the rattling instead of the light. Warfare in the mind often sounds like that door's noise without substance, shadows without form, accusations with no evidence. Real warfare, the kind that actually matters, is always tied to movement. It shows up when you walk toward the doors, spilling light, when you step into new territory, and when you advance into healing and purpose. That's when the enemy panics. He hates momentum. He hates forward motion. He hates it when women get free and start lighting torches for the next one.

You have all the power in this hallway. Every step you take is an announcement to hell that you are not turning back. Every door you walk past—the ones that rattle and hiss—loses authority over you simply because you chose not to open it. And every door of light you walk toward expands your courage, strengthens your mind, and aligns your heart with the truth about who you are.

I want you to hear me say this plainly: I am preaching to myself right now. I am writing this part of the book from the middle of my own hallway. Every time I have tried to release this book, every time I have tried to write or teach or take one more step toward helping you heal, warfare has broken out. I have faced resistance so intense at times that it felt like it came out of nowhere. The enemy has tried to convince me that I am not ready, that I am not qualified, that I am too broken, too busy, too overwhelmed, too anything. But I finally realized that this—this specific push back—is the proof. It is the evidence that what I am carrying will set captives free.

Sharing our testimony is a blow the enemy cannot recover from. It is Jaels' tent peg and hammer, straight into the temple of the enemy. Every time a survivor opens her mouth and tells the truth about what God has done, hell loses territory. The enemy can tempt, rattle, accuse, intimidate—but he cannot undo a testimony. He cannot un-resurrect what God has healed. He cannot erase the places where God has redeemed the story.

So I am doing the exact same thing you are doing. I am walking forward. I am passing by the rattling doors. I am choosing the light. I am pushing through the hallway knowing that someone else's life is tied to my obedience. And you need to know that someone else's life is tied to yours, too. Not under pressure... but on purpose. Your freedom will unlock someone else's courage. Your healing will become someone else's map. Your voice will become someone else's weapon.

And together, step by step, story by story, we will take the territory back.

5

Chapter 5: From Broken to Beautiful

After learning about spiritual warfare, think of it as the enemy capturing the flag of a territory—our mind, will, emotions, and spirit. If this feels intense or new, that's okay. Everyone connects with these ideas in their own way and at their own pace. Wherever you are on your journey, you are welcome here. Today, we take back our ground. We step into our God-given identity and declare victory over every lie that tried to define us. Join me in this decree of truth over yourself before we begin.

I declare that I, _________________________________, was born for a time such as this, with a mighty purpose. Jesus is my light and my salvation; whom shall I fear? I rejoice because God has rescued me ___________________. I will sing to Abba, for He has been good to me. Even when my earthly father or mother or others rejected me, He received me. He is not a reflection of them but the perfection of a good Father.

The Holy Spirit is my forever friend, nurturing me like a mother—gentle, kind, and full of love that endures forever. He is healing my heart and binding my wounds. He reached from the ends of the earth, from the farthest corners, and called me _________________. I will not fear vulnerability with Him, because He is my refuge and strong tower. I will rest by still waters, drinking from His living water.

My body is safe in Abba's hands. He protects me and came to give me an abundant life. I speak abundant life over every part of my body—from head to toe—every organ, system, blood cell, bone, muscle, and cartilage, purified by the blood poured out on the cross for me _________________. By His stripes, I am healed!

I continually receive with open arms an abundance of grace and the gift of righteousness. I will reign in this life through Jesus living in me. I am a daughter of the King, and my inheritance is to experience heaven here on earth. He loves me because He loves me because He loves me.

Because this is truth, I encourage you to screenshot these pages or write them down and declare them over yourself every day.

I'm excited to explore your original design with you! But before we start, let's take a moment to worship together. I picked the song No Fear in Love by Steffany Gretzinger because it's a perfect way to help you reconnect with yourself—the girl, teen, or woman you were before the abuse and its effects.

If you can't play the song right now, that's okay. You can sing softly, praise Him, or simply speak your heart to God. Worship is a powerful way to create space for the Holy Spirit to guide you back to your original design.

Some of the lyrics that really resonate are:

There's no fear in love. "Stir in me a love that's deep, wide, and sweet, and help me, Lord, to never keep it to myself."

"And if my heart should dimly burn, and if my feet should fail to run, call my name, and I will come right back to You."

What a beautiful song. Let that truth sink in. God's love is always greater than anything you've faced. Even in moments of fear, pain, or confusion, He is calling you back to who you were created to be. Enough is enough. After recognizing all that's been lost or stolen, you might feel unsure about what comes next. Maybe you're like I was, new to the idea of original design. That's okay! Remember, the enemy came to steal, kill, and destroy, but God came to give abundant life. Your original design is meant to be filled with that abundant life.

I used to believe the struggles, like the anxiety, shame, and behaviors that didn't feel like me, were simply who I was. I thought God designed me to be chubby as a child. I thought my personality quirks were just "me." But as I began to heal and reflect, I realized many of these things were not part of my original design. They were survival mechanisms, adaptations to abuse, and learned trauma behaviors.

If you don't remember your early years or aren't sure who you were before the trauma, know that this is completely normal. Memory gaps are common in healing from trauma, and they don't mean you can't heal or find your true self. Healing is possible even without clear memories.

So how do you start discovering your original design? The first step is to pray. Invite the Holy Spirit to guide you on this journey. This isn't a one-time thing. Keep asking Him to reveal who Abba created you to be. Before you sleep, declare dreams and visions over yourself. Trust that what He shows you will reflect His character because you were made in His image. Then, think back to your younger years. If you have trusted loved ones, ask them what you were like before the abuse or trauma. It's okay if you don't have this info—I didn't, since my abuse started as an infant. Still, the Holy Spirit can show you glimpses of who you really were—what brought you joy, what you loved, and how you connected with the world.

For example, growing up, I swore I would never have kids. Initially, I didn't want them. However, years later, the Holy Spirit reminded me of a little baby doll I carried everywhere as a young girl. Through this memory, I recognized that I had a natural, nurturing spirit I had buried beneath fear. With this insight, my outlook on parenting completely transformed. Suddenly, I realized that this desire to nurture had always been part of me, even if it had been overshadowed by fear for so long.

Similarly, the Holy Spirit gradually returned memories, piecing together who I was before fear. He reminded me of my love for show-and-tell at school. The joy of sharing, being seen and heard, never left me—it was just buried under trauma. This joy is what this book and journey are about: reclaiming and expressing your true self.

Remember, finding your original design is not about perfection. It is about rediscovering the essence of who God made you to be. He has been with you all along, even in the moments of fear, pain, and confusion. He is gently restoring the pieces of your heart that were hidden or stolen, and as you walk this journey, He will reveal the fullness of your original design, piece by piece.

So, how do you discover your original design? First, pray. Invite the Holy Spirit to join you in this journey. This is not just a lesson or one-time event. Keep asking Him to reveal who Abba created you to be. Before you go to sleep, speak dreams and visions over your original design, knowing that what He shows you will always align with His character because you were made in His image.

Next, think back to your younger years. If you have trusted

loved ones, ask them what you were like before the abuse or trauma occurred. It's okay if you don't have access to this information. I didn't, as I began being abused as an infant. Even so, you can invite the Holy Spirit, and He will begin showing you glimpses of what truly brought you joy.

For example, growing up, I swore I would never have kids, as I mentioned above. I didn't want them. But that was really a facade to cover a fear of intimacy. When I wrote this section, I was pregnant with my fourth child, and the Holy Spirit reminded me of a little baby I carried everywhere as a young girl. I had a natural nurturing in me, a desire for babies. My entire outlook on parenting changed since then. I have always loved my kids, but suddenly it felt like parenting was ingrained in me, that it had always been a part of my original design.

The Holy Spirit slowly began bringing memories back to me, like piecing together parts of who I was as a child before fear took over—kind of like *Finding Dory*. One of my favorite things He reminded me of was how much I loved doing show-and-tell at school. That joy of sharing is what this book is about: rediscovering yourself and showing your true self to the world.

He also reminded me of my style. This might sound silly, but I realized I could just be myself. I love the beach, and I'm sporty by design. I stopped trying to follow trends and decided to be me. Most days, you'll find me in casual beach clothes and sandals. He even showed me my original hair color! For years, I dyed my hair trying to fit in. After having my first son, people asked where he got his hair color, and I had no idea. So I stopped dyeing my hair to see what would happen. I can't tell you how much I love my natural hair now and how many compliments I get. Turns out, my original design is pretty cool!

God has highlighted all the ways He created me and how much

He loves them. He has shown me that I actually like dresses and it's okay to feel like His princess. He has shown me my love for writing, speaking, teaching, and praying—even though I wasn't raised around God, I can always remember praying to Him. He has shown me that I love physical exercise and that I was created to compete—not against others, but against the enemy. He has shown me that I secretly enjoy being introverted at times, even though I love community and tend to be extroverted. He has reminded me that I love watching birds, being a mom and wife, painting, and worship. He even showed me His original design for me during childbirth, which led to an all-natural, pain-free birth. Seriously, Heaven on Earth is real, and His original design is so fun!

So please be encouraged as you discover your original design. Take some time today to rest, journal, and reflect on what the Holy Spirit is showing you. It's completely normal if you find it hard to hear God's voice or if it feels distant or unclear sometimes. That doesn't mean there's anything wrong with you or that you can't heal. Healing can happen even when God's presence feels quiet or hard to grasp. His voice is different for everyone. Some hear Him through music, memories, nature, the Word, sermons, friends, children, art, dreams, prophetic words, or quiet moments. He is always speaking, and the Holy Spirit is always revealing who He is.

Remember, His yoke is easy, and His burden is light. If it feels heavy, pause, soak in His presence, and worship.

Now that you've spent some time reflecting with the Holy Spirit, we are going to take what you've discovered and declare it with the renewing of our minds. Romans 12:2 says:

"Do not conform to the pattern of this world, but be transformed by the renewing of your mind. Then you will be able to test and

approve what God's will is—his good, pleasing, and perfect will."

Renewing your mind is key to returning to your original design. Remember, we can intentionally rewire our thoughts. Here's a story from my life: I once thought fear, worry, and anxiety were part of my original design. But they weren't. Those feelings were habits I picked up from the environment I grew up in. Over time, my brain got used to going down those paths of fear and anxiety.

Through prayer, reflection, and the guidance of the Holy Spirit, I began to reverse engineer those thought patterns. I chose to replace fear with faith, worry with trust, and anxiety with peace. This is how you reclaim your original design—you actively renew your mind and align your thoughts with God's truth.

This journey is ongoing, and it will continue to reveal deeper parts of who you were created to be. Be patient with yourself. Celebrate the little glimpses, the small victories, and the reminders of joy. Each revelation is a step back into the life God always intended for you—a life of freedom, peace, and the fullness of your original design.

One of the strongest effects of sexual abuse I experienced was hypochondria. It was a fear that completely took over my mind, and I had to intentionally work on it to renew my thoughts and reclaim my original design.

I want to break down how I completely overcame this fear and renewed my mind.

First, I had to make sure what I fed my mind matched my goal of overcoming hypochondria. That meant choosing carefully what I watched and read. I stopped watching medical shows like *Grey's Anatomy*, stopped googling every symptom I felt, and stopped reading all the scary stories and tragic testimonies online.

Next, I cultivated an atmosphere of faith around this struggle. I began reading testimonies of people who had overcome hypochondria, surrounding myself with the victory I wanted to experience. You can do this with any area of your life where you need to renew your mind.

Then, I invited the Holy Spirit to guide me. I offered this area as a sacrifice to Jesus, surrendering it at His feet. I knew that the only way I could overcome this was by being led by His power.

I also learned from Dr. Caroline Leaf, a Christian brain scientist, that it takes 63 days to form a new neural pathway. I decided to intentionally renew my mind for 63 days. I learned it only takes seven minutes a day to start creating that new pathway.

The Holy Spirit gave me a great idea: He said, "Syl, why don't you record my promises over yourself in a seven-minute voice recording?" So I did. I found it really powerful to hear my own voice declaring these promises because sometimes, when my mind was struggling, I needed to hear myself say them to believe them.

He also introduced me to the **PP Factor: Pause and Party.** Not a crazy party, but a Holy Spirit party. Anytime a scary thought about my body would pop up, I would literally pause and sing a brilliant chant the Holy Spirit gave me:

Give me an L...L, you got that L, you got that L Give me an I...I, you got that I, you got that I

Give me an F...F, you got that F, you got that F

Give me an E....E, you got that E, you got that E

What does that spell? LIFE! Abundantly! He gives life abundantly! He's here to set me free with His life abundantly!

I am thrilled to say I no longer struggle with hypochondria at all—after 34 years of living in that fear! But hypochondria is not the only area in which I have had to overcome fear in my life. There were many.

Before moving on to the next part of this book, pick **one area of your life** where you want to renew your mind and get back to your original design. Do this for 63 days and watch how God works. If you miss a day or struggle to keep up, know that healing isn't a straight line and there's no "perfect" way to go through this process. You don't have to start over. Just pick up where you left off, and be gentle and kind with yourself. Everyone moves at their own pace, and that's totally okay.

Be sure to check the resources tab for more information on renewing your mind. I've included declaration templates that you can record over your life. I highly recommend recording them in your own voice. There is something powerful about speaking God's truth over yourself—your spirit recognizes it, and your mind begins to follow.

Activating the Renewal of Your Mind Through Your Senses

One of the most powerful ways to renew your mind is by intentionally activating it through your senses and imagination. Our minds are designed to process the world around us, and when trauma or abuse has hijacked certain pathways, we can redirect them toward healing and life.

Think of your imagination like a womb. What you imagine, you give birth to in your life. This is why the Bible tells us to meditate on things that are true, noble, right, pure, lovely, admirable, excellent, and praiseworthy (Philippians 4:8). What we imagine becomes the blueprint for what we live. So what are we going to imagine? Are we going to keep recreating fear, shame, and trauma? Or are we going to intentionally imagine freedom, joy, identity, and love?

Here's how you can activate your mind through the senses:

1. Visual:

Use your imagination to create mental "movies" of the life God designed for you. Picture yourself walking in confidence, speaking truth, enjoying relationships, and moving freely in your body. You can also use vision boards, sketches, or doodles to give your imagination a tangible outlet. One of my favorite practices is to close my eyes and let the Holy Spirit guide me through a visual meditation of myself as the girl I was created to be—safe, strong, and loved.

2. Hearing:

Sound directly affects the mind and emotions. Worship, prayer, and even your own voice declaring God's promises can rewire your thoughts. Remember the chant I shared earlier for hypochondria? Hearing yourself speak truth to your mind connects with your brain in ways outside words can't. I still listen to a 20-minute recording of myself declaring truth over my life and future. They say it takes 7 minutes a day to build a new pathway, so I take that seriously, especially when I'm struggling. Just recently, I was in a funk while finishing this book, and God told me to listen to the song I AM NO VICTIM on repeat as I walked 5 miles. That hour and 20 minutes of meditation helped shift me out of a victim mindset. Sometimes we have to take radical responsibility. Listening to uplifting music, sermons, or affirmations that match your original design will help build new thought pathways.

3. Smell:

Smell is strongly linked to memory and emotion. Certain scents can trigger peace, comfort, or joy. When I was in intense healing, I would light candles or use essential oils while praying or journal. That scent became associated with God's presence, safety, and restoration. Every time I smelled it afterward, my brain and spirit were reminded of His care.

4. Touch and Movement:

Your body holds memory, too. Movement, stretching, exercise, or simply placing your hands over your heart while praying can reinforce new neurological pathways and shift your body from a fight-or-flight state to one of calm and receptivity. Even small physical actions like holding a journal or a meaningful object while meditating can anchor your mind in new, healthy patterns.

5. Imagination as a Womb:

The imagination is where ideas are conceived. What we dwell on grows. Sexual abuse survivors often have to renew their minds in very specific areas because abuse distorts perceptions of safety, self-worth, boundaries, and love. We have to intentionally "imagine" these areas healed and restored. Later, what we imagine shapes our thoughts, emotions, and ultimately our reality.

Here are the **most common areas sexual abuse survivors need to renew their minds in**, along with practical steps:

a. Safety in Your Body:

- Visualize yourself protected by a loving presence.
- Use affirmations like, *"My body is a temple of the Holy Spirit. I am safe."*
- Move intentionally through your body, noticing sensations, and release tension with breath and prayer.

b. Worth and Identity:

- Journal or speak aloud: "I a*m beloved. I am chosen. I am whole in Christ.*"
- Imagine the little girl you once were embracing herself fully, loved and affirmed.

c. Fear and Anxiety:

- Use imagination to create a "safe space" in your mind—a room, a garden, a beach—where you can retreat for prayer and reflection.
- Pair this with Scripture or worship music that speaks peace over you.

d. Shame and Guilt:

- Speak truth over yourself: *"The blood of Jesus covers me. I am forgiven. I am not defined by what was done to me."*
- Imagine cutting cords or chains in your mind that represent shame.

e. Control and Trust:

- Practice surrender through guided imagination—imagine handing over the burden, worry, or fear to God.
- Use your senses: see it, feel it, hear it being lifted off your shoulders.

f. Intimacy and Love:

Picture safe relationships, hugs, laughter, and joy. Hear yourself saying, *"I am worthy of love. I am lovable. I can receive good things."*

The key is **repetition and intentionality**. As you engage your senses and imagination, your brain starts to rewrite old patterns, reinforcing the life and original design God has placed within you. Every sensory experience, every visualization, every declaration about yourself builds pathways back to freedom and wholeness.

Remember, the enemy wants to keep you trapped in the old narrative, but the Holy Spirit will guide you into new thoughts and dreams. Let your imagination be the womb of your restoration.

I didn't plan on putting this into the book—this is something I usually give to my clients in the ARISE Course—but here are some journal prompts to help you start the renewing of your mind process.

Each day focuses on one area, using imagination, Scripture, and intentional sensory exercises to rewire thought patterns and reinforce your identity in Christ.

Day 1: Declare Your Safety

- **Scripture Focus:** Psalm 91:1
- -2 – *"He who dwells in the secret place of the Most High shall abide under the shadow of the Almighty."*

Exercise:

1. Find a quiet space. Close your eyes and take deep breaths.
2. Imagine a protective light surrounding your body. Feel it covering every part of you.
3. Speak out loud: *"I am safe. My body is a temple of the Holy Spirit. No harm can overtake me."*
4. Optional: Light a candle or use a comforting scent to anchor

this visualization.

Day 2: Reclaim Your Identity

- **Scripture Focus:** Ephesians 1:4-5 – *"He chose us before the foundation of the world to be holy and blameless before Him."*
- *Exercise:* Write down three words that describe your God-given identity.

1. Visualize the little girl you were before trauma and imagine her embraced by God.
2. Speak these words over yourself: *"I am beloved, chosen, whole in Christ."*

Day 3: Release Fear and Anxiety

- **Scripture Focus:** 2 Timothy 1:7 – *"For God has not given us a spirit of fear, but of power, love, and a sound mind."*

Exercise:

1. Close your eyes and picture a safe space—a garden, a beach, or a room.
2. Imagine placing your fears and anxieties into a box in this space. Speak aloud: *"Lord, I surrender my fears to You. I trust Your guidance and protection."*

Day 4: Break Shame and Guilt

- **Scripture Focus:**

- Romans 8:1 – *"There is now no condemnation for those who are in Christ Jesus."*

Exercise:

1. Write down any shame or guilt you are carrying.
2. Pray over each one, saying: *"By the blood of Jesus, I am forgiven. I am free."*
3. Tear the paper, burn it safely, or symbolically release it to God.

Day 5: Strengthen Trust and Control

- **Scripture Focus:** Proverbs
- 3:5-6 – *"Trust in the Lord with all your heart and lean not on your own understanding."*

Exercise:

1. Visualize yourself handing over control to God. Imagine your worries and burdens being lifted from your shoulders. Speak aloud: *"Lord, I trust You to lead me. I surrender my will to Your good plan."*
2. Journal any thoughts or feelings that come up.

Day 6: Embrace Love and Intimacy

- **Scripture Focus:** 1 John 4:18 – *"There is no fear in love. Perfect love drives out fear."*

Exercise:

1. Close your eyes and picture safe, loving relationships.
2. Imagine laughter, hugs, joy, and emotional safety.
3. Speak aloud: *"I am worthy of love. I am lovable. I can receive good things."*
4. Optional: Play uplifting worship music to strengthen the atmosphere of love.

Day 7: Celebrate Your Original Design

- **Scripture Focus:** Psalm 139:13-14 – *"For You created my inmost being; You knit me together in my mother's womb. I praise You because I am fearfully and wonderfully made."*
- **Exercise:**Reflect on all the things you've discovered about your original design this week.

1. Make a list of your God-given gifts, passions, and strengths.
2. Speak aloud a declaration over your life:

I am fearfully and wonderfully made. I am walking in my original design. I receive joy, love, and freedom in every area of my life."

Optional: Celebrate with worship, movement, or a creative outlet like art, journaling, or music.

Extra Tips

- Repeat any day as needed. The Holy Spirit will guide you to areas that need more attention.
- Engage multiple senses: visualize, speak, touch meaningful objects, listen to worship music, and breathe intentionally.
- Keep a journal to track progress, insights, and revelations. This will serve as a tangible reminder of your transforma-

tion.

6

Chapter 6: Soul Delving, Healing the Hidden You

You are halfway through the Arise course, and I want to begin by honoring you. You are courageous for coming this far. It takes bravery to face the journey of healing, and I see your commitment and strength. I'm thrilled for this milestone. Friends, I love every part of this journey, but this chapter is my favorite. This section was life-changing for my healing. If I had only accessed this chapter, I'd have paid a million dollars— it would have shortened my journey. That's why I'm writing this book: to help your healing go faster. God commissioned me to guide you and accelerate your freedom.

This chapter focuses on your soul—the part of you carrying the weight of the past. Abuse, trauma, fear, and pain leave marks that affect your emotions, choices, relationships, and purpose. The good news? God designed your soul to be resilient, healed, and restored. Here, you'll learn to tend your soul, understand its needs, and walk in the freedom God intended. If spiritual warfare arises as you read, decide now: *I win. I will finish this chapter.* Your victory depends on God's power, your surrender,

75

and your willingness to believe who He says you are.

Pause here. This time, use thanksgiving as a weapon. Take a moment to list three things you're grateful for—speak them out loud or write them down. Thanksgiving is a spiritual tool that shifts your focus and opens your heart to God's presence. Declare: *Holy Spirit, silence the enemy. Bind my mind to Christ. I walk in Your freedom, guidance, and truth. Breathe deeply.* Prepare your heart. Your soul is about to be awakened, healed, and restored.

We are wired to crave His presence. We have an insatiable hunger that only His love and presence can fill. Trying to fill that space with people, addictions, or distractions makes our souls malfunction. Abuse, trauma, and neglect can create anxiety, depression, OCD, bipolar disorder, self-destruction, lust, and more. Our souls cry out for the living water of God, but we use substitutes. I'll share a deeply personal season from my life to teach about the soul's role in healing. This journey began after my first son's birth—I faced every type of postpartum depression. It was horrific and overwhelming. If someone had told me then that I'd lead women, free from postpartum depression and anxiety, I wouldn't have believed them.

Postpartum depression was a surface symptom. The root was deep—tangled trauma and abuse. True healing meant going past body and mind into the soul. Ten months in, I started reflecting and combining medical knowledge with faith. I asked: What tugs at my soul? What triggers make postpartum feel like trauma? Here's what I found: we are tri-beings—body, soul, and spirit. The body is our earthly vessel; it doesn't follow us when we leave. The soul is our mind, will, emotions, and conscience. Our spirit is made for connection; it's our spiritual Wi-Fi to God and eternity.

So let's talk more about our soul. You've probably heard this term a million times, and I had too—but I never understood how much it affects every area of life. Dallas Willard explains it beautifully when he says, "Our *soul is like a stream of water, which gives strength, direction, and harmony to every other area of our life. When that stream is as it should be, we are constantly refreshed and exuberant in all we do, because our soul itself is then profusely rooted in the vastness of God and His kingdom, including nature, and all else within us is enlivened and directed by that stream. Therefore, we are in harmony with God, reality, and the rest of human nature and nature at large.*"

Picture this: your soul is an inner stream, giving life to every part of you. When it flows freely, you are refreshed and joyful. But life happens. Trauma, abuse, and loss block the stream with unresolved pain and wounds.

These blockages cause stagnation and contamination. That's why trauma and neglect show up as anxiety, depression, fear, anger, addiction, and countless struggles. Your soul is not meant to hold this weight but to process, heal, and flow in harmony with God. That's what we dive into this chapter: Soul Delving— Healing the Hidden You. We will uncover wounds, identify blockages, and restore the living water.

Realizing how much my soul was affected was eye-opening. The postpartum depression was tangled with decades of trauma and abuse. My emotions were erratic, my mind raced, and my will was exhausted. I carried a heavy load I didn't know existed. But God showed me I could tend to my soul, clear the debris, and restore the living water. This isn't an overnight fix. It takes patience, intentionality, and guidance from the Holy Spirit. The stream is alive. As we tend to it—through prayer, worship, reflection, journaling, and surrender—transformation ripples through body, soul, and spirit.

Next, we will explore practical ways to tend your soul, identify blockages, and cultivate flow. Here is where hidden healing work happens—and it's worth every step. Imagine you scored your dream mountain property. A clear stream, teeming with rainbow trout, ran through it. The stream thrived thanks to an amazing caretaker who managed all the local properties. After any storm or issue, he would arrive, clear the aftermath, remove debris, and take preventive steps to address future challenges. He excelled at his work. Now, let's pretend your husband (haha, because it would never be us, right? Wink wink) decided the stream keeper's awesomeness didn't fit the budget. He thought the stream could take care of itself—it's part of nature, right? Fast forward to Memorial Day weekend. You plan to relax at the property, but arrive at a mess: twigs and branches everywhere, muddy, low water, compacted silt, and stagnant sections. Wildlife is gone, the air is stale, and even the kids have lost interest. Neighbors get sick from the stagnant water. The stream is now harmed by neglect.

It becomes obvious—you need to rehire the stream keeper. Once he returns, everything changes: the water runs crisp and clear, the air smells like a glacier meadow, wildlife reappears, and kids fish and swim again. Life and vitality are restored. This perfectly pictures us. The stream is your soul; the keeper is you in partnership with the Holy Spirit. During my postpartum season, realizing this felt like a blindfold lifted—I saw clearly for the first time. My soul harbored trauma, abuse, abandonment, grief, and more. These weren't just hormonal shifts but layers of life events clogging my inner stream.

This might feel like a lot, maybe even out of nowhere. You may wonder if this relates to your healing now. I get it. It is completely normal to feel overwhelmed, numb, resistant, or even frustrated as you walk through these deeper layers. These emotional reactions are not a sign that anything is wrong with you—in fact, they are part of the healing journey itself. Most of us instinctively avoid hard stuff, so remembering takes time and sometimes feels uncomfortable. Please know that whatever you are feeling, you are not alone and you are not failing. Your emotions, even the difficult ones, are actually signals that your soul is waking up and beginning to process and release what it has carried for so long. Give yourself permission to feel what you feel, and know that pressing through is an act of great courage. I encourage you: keep walking the journey. Finish each phase of this book. Your soul has everything to gain. Science struggles to understand the soul. Much of what happens after trauma is labeled as a bodily or psychological disorder. But this misses the soul's role. We develop coping habits to survive, often unknowingly. The soul can't run alone. It's like a router with no connection; it needs God, through the Holy Spirit.

During my postpartum season, I realized that what I was experiencing was happening in my mind—thoughts, worries, anxieties—yet these were symptoms of the deeper workings of my soul: mind, will, emotions, and conscience. Digging deep into my soul became the turning point of my healing journey. It was the step that ultimately led me from surviving to living in complete victory. HEALING FROM WITHIN

For a long time, I did not understand the depth of what was happening inside me. I knew I struggled with anger, and I knew I struggled with depression, but I did not yet understand that these were not isolated behaviors. They were symptoms of a deeper wound in my soul.

There was a season of my life when my reactions would come

so quickly that I could not catch them. I would explode before I even knew what I was doing. The shame that followed felt unbearable. When my husband and I were dating, he told me gently but honestly that I needed anger management. At the time, it felt humiliating. I thought it meant something was permanently wrong with me. Looking back, I see that those words were not meant to wound me. They were the beginning of my healing because they forced me to look within.

On the other side of those outbursts, I experienced the opposite extreme. A deep sinking that felt like falling into a pit where I could barely hold on. I reached moments where I did not want to be alive. Functioning felt like climbing uphill with no strength left. Everything was heavy, and everything was hard. Both the rage and the depression grew worse when I stopped drinking and laid down the addictions I had used as a crutch. Sobriety can feel like stripping away the surface layer, and suddenly, you are face-to-face with the rawness of your own soul.

After some time, I began studying Hebraic thought. Not as a magical cure but as a way of understanding the deeper patterns of the heart. In ancient Hebrew, every letter carries a picture and a meaning. That language has a way of revealing truths we cannot always articulate. When I learned how anger and depression are viewed in Hebraic symbolism, something inside me softened.

The Hebrew word for anger is aph. It is made of Aleph and Peh. Aleph is the picture of a strong leader. It conveys a sense of fatherly strength and protection. Peh is the picture of the mouth and expression. When anger rises uncontrollably, it can be seen in these symbols as the father's strength erupting from the mouth without guidance or grounding. It asks the soul a question that I never stopped long enough to hear. Where was the fathering presence that steadies and protects? Where was the sense of strength that teaches you how to hold yourself from within?

Depression reveals a different picture. In Hebrew symbolism, it is often connected to the letter Mem. Mem is the image of water, the womb, and the nurturing presence of the mother. It represents the emotional place where we are held, soothed, and supported. When that nurture is disrupted or when it was never deeply formed in childhood, the soul can collapse inward. Depression becomes the question beneath the heaviness. Where was the mothering presence? Where was the emotional safety that told you you were supported and not alone?

These are not literal dictionary translations, but they are deeply faithful to the heart of Hebraic pictographs. They offer a way of seeing the soul that goes beneath the surface. For me, they opened a door. The rage was not a sign that I was beyond repair. It was the cry of an unprotected part of me. The depression was not a weakness. It was the ache of an unheld part of me. When I understood this, my healing no longer felt like punishment. It felt like tending to a child inside me who had gone unseen for too long.

This is the invitation of soul delving. To sit with what rises. To let the truth reveal itself in layers. To let God step into the places where fathering was absent and mothering was fragile. Healing began when I allowed Him to be both strength and nurture for the parts of me that had never known either. And slowly my reactions softened. My emotions settled. My inner world learned to breathe again.

If you are reading this and recognizing pieces of yourself, know this. Nothing is wrong with you. You are not broken. You are simply being invited into a deeper understanding of your own soul. There is healing available. There is restoration available. And there is a God who knows how to meet you in every place where you were once left alone.

THE SOUL OF A CHILD

How Hebrew Thought Reveals What Our Hearts Already Know. When we begin to trace the roots of our wounds, we must go back to the soul. Scripture describes the soul with the Hebrew word nephesh, and the more I learned about this word, the more my own story began to make sense. In Hebrew thought, the soul of a child is tender, open, and unformed. It is the part of us that breathes, desires, feels, and absorbs the world long before we have language to describe it. Genesis says that God breathed into Adam, and he became a living nephesh, a living soul. This breath is the very core of who we are.

What makes this so important, especially for those of us who experienced trauma, is the Hebrew understanding that a child's soul is shaped before it can speak. Proverbs teaches that a child's heart is unformed and needs guidance. The Hebrew word for heart, levav, is not just about emotion. It is the place of direction and identity. What enters a child's heart at an early age becomes the structure they will live from as adults. This is why Proverbs says to train up a child in the way he should go, because early shaping becomes a lifelong pattern.

Ancient Hebrew thought also describes the yetzer, a person's inner inclination. A child is believed to have only the yetzer ra, the impulsive, unregulated instinct to react. The yetzer tov, the inclination toward maturity and self-governance, comes much later. This is not sinfulness. It is incompleteness. A child cannot carry what an adult carries. A child was never meant to regulate fear, betrayal, or chaos alone. Scripture affirms this again when it tells us that folly is bound up in the heart of a child, meaning simply that the inner world is unshaped. Children are raw souls, and they borrow stability from the adults around them.

This brings us to one of the most profound truths: in Hebrew thought, the soul of a child is held within the souls of the parents. A child receives strength from a father's presence and safety from a mother's nurture. This imagery appears again and again. The father is described as the one who establishes identity and instruction. The mother is portrayed as the one who comforts, soothes, and holds. Isaiah says that God comforts His people as a mother comforts her child. The Psalms speak of being weaned like a child resting against its mother. These pictures reveal the soul's deep structure. When fathering is absent, the soul becomes untethered. When mothering is fragile, the soul becomes unheld.

For many of us, this is where fragmentation occurs. Trauma can freeze parts of the soul at the age when the wound happened. Modern psychology calls this the inner child. Hebrew thought simply recognized that parts of the soul can be broken, over-whelmed, or dissociated. The Psalmist cried, Restore my soul. The Hebrew word for restore also means to repair and to bring back what has been lost. The soul can fracture, and the soul can be restored.

I believe deeply that we can get stuck spending our entire lives trying to parent the fragments within us. We nurture the inner child, we soothe the younger version of ourselves, we maintain the wounded places. There is nothing wrong with these tools, but they can keep us circling around the injury without ever moving into maturity. What modern psychology often stops short of proclaiming is what Scripture reveals with clarity. There comes a moment when the Holy Spirit touches a fractured place in the soul, and healing can come in a single breath.

This does not erase the process, nor does it mean we will never revisit memories, but it does mean that healing is not earned by effort. Healing happens when the veil is pulled back, and God walks with us into the places we have long avoided. The memories that surface are not for our pain but for our freedom. When God brings something back to your remembrance, He is not trying to hurt you. He is leading you into truth so that truth can make you free.

Not long ago, I experienced this in a way that shook me. I was sitting quietly, listening to my declarations, allowing my spirit to settle. Out of nowhere, the Holy Spirit brought back a memory I had never fully processed. Years ago, court paperwork revealed an account from a witness connected to the abuse that happened with my biological father. She had written down what I told her as a child. Those words described him pointing to airplanes and telling me that if I ever spoke about what he had done, he would push my mother and grandmother off the plane so they would die.

Before I ever knew that memory existed, my soul reacted. For years, I had panic attacks at the sight of airplanes. My body would tremble, and my heart would race. I did not understand it logically, but my soul remembered what my mind had forgotten. Trauma had frozen something inside me at the age when that threat was spoken.

But when the Holy Spirit brought that memory to the surface, something else happened. I saw the belief I had carried ever since childhood. I believed I was responsible for saving my mother and grandmother. I carried the weight of their safety as a little girl, and that burden grew into fear, hypervigilance, and a soul always bracing for loss. That was the stronghold, and it lived in the deepest place of my nephesh.

But here is the truth. The moment God revealed it, He began to heal it. Not through years of managing my inner child. Not through endlessly revisiting the wound. But through a single moment of revelation. The veil was lifted, and light entered the part of my soul that had been frozen in fear. Scripture says that the Lord is near to the brokenhearted and saves those crushed in spirit. I felt that I saved work in an instant. The broken part of me was no longer abandoned. God Himself stepped into the memory, not to reopen it, but to release me from it.

These are the places He is taking you back to. Not so you can relive the hurt, but so you can walk in freedom. What your soul remembers, God intends to redeem. What trauma fractured, He intends to restore. The healing of your memories is not regression. It is resurrection. And the same Spirit that raised Jesus from the dead is restoring every part of your soul that life tried to bury.

NOW THAT YOU UNDERSTAND YOUR SOUL, LET US BEGIN THE HEALING

Now that you understand what has been happening inside you, I want to take you into a moment of activation and healing. You have spent these pages gaining language for the movements of your soul, but now it is time to experience the restoration for which you were created. Wouldn't it be incredible if, in the next few minutes, the veil lifted and your soul shifted the same way mine did? It truly can happen. But before we take that step, I want you to remember what we talked about in our spiritual warfare chapter. If suddenly you feel tired, distracted, anxious, irritated, or overwhelmed, pause. Do not disconnect. Do not put this book away and promise yourself you will come back later.

You declared your why earlier, and right now, you are choosing to stand on that decision.

If panic rises or uneasiness creeps in, understand that it is a mirage from the enemy. Open Psalm 91. Read it out loud. Say the name of Jesus with authority. Speak to the enemy and tell him he has no place in your mind, your atmosphere, or your healing. You are stepping into sacred ground right now. You are choosing to be healed.

So I am going to ask you to do something with me. Be brave.

When I think of the word brave, I immediately picture a mama bear: fierce, protective, and willing to do anything for her young. Even if you are not a mother, you have that same God-given instinct within you—a protective fierceness that can rise up when someone or something you love is threatened. Sometimes trauma buries it, but it is never lost. That same instinct is what calls you to be courageous in your own healing journey.

Let your soul rise with that protective love. Step into the deep places of healing with courage instead of fear. This is part of your journey to arise.

(Whenever you see me reference my "mama bear instinct" in later chapters, I am drawing on this fierce, protective love—the same one that can help you fight for your own soul's healing.)

As I shared earlier, my own healing began when I realized that the postpartum depression had deeper roots than hormones or exhaustion. I saw how my soul had been impacted by the abuse, abandonment, and grief I had never fully addressed. Once I began learning about the Body, Soul, and Spirit, everything started to make sense. The depression was not just physical. It was soul deep. My soul was sending signals my mind did not yet recognize.

But even with that understanding, I avoided dealing with those wounds. I was exhausted. The idea of unpacking trauma sounded like more emotional labor than I could bear. I was working on my body at the time, focusing on nutrition and wellness, and the soul felt like the last thing I wanted to touch.

Until one day, something shifted. I realized that the trauma affecting my soul was not only shaping me. It was shaping my child, my future children, the longevity of my life, my friendships, my marriage, my joy, and every relationship I cared about. Something fierce awakened inside me. My mama bear instinct rose up. I decided to be brave, not just for myself, but for every life connected to mine.

And I am so grateful I did. Three children later, my life and my postpartum seasons have never been more healed, more grounded, or more full of peace.

So what did I do first? I remembered what I taught you in part one. We are tri beings. Body, Soul, Spirit. Healing does not happen in one dimension. It flows through all three.

My first step was choosing to believe in what I could not see. We have never seen our true body, only its reflection in a mirror, yet we trust that reflection when it shows us mascara smudged under our eye or lettuce in our teeth. The soul is easier to recognize. If someone speaks harshly, you feel the sting, not in your body but in your inner world. That is the soul.

The spirit is different. You cannot touch it or see it, much like you cannot see WiFi, yet the signal allows you to access unlimited information. The human spirit works the same way. Something unseen influences everything you think, feel, and experience.

As I walked deeper into healing, I realized the things influencing my spirit were not feeding life. I was letting social media shape my identity, letting movies and music tether themselves to my emotions, letting entertainment become the voice discipling my inner world. What flows into your spirit eventually flows into your soul, and what flows into your soul eventually manifests in your body. All three were crying out for help.

I was at rock bottom, and I needed help. I was beginning to face the truth that there were layers in my soul I had never dared to look at. Trust me, I know how difficult this is. My soul was carrying extreme physical, sexual, and verbal abuse from my own father. It held deaths in the family, the wounds of an addicted parent, the instability of a stepdad who was hurting and deeply militant and verbally abusive, and the long list of poor choices I made throughout my adolescent years that opened the door to even more sexual traumas. My soul was a battlefield, and for the first time, I was starting to see how much it needed rescue.

As you read this, I want you to pause and softly acknowledge this truth. If my soul could hold so much and still find healing, your soul can too. Your story may look different from mine, but every soul carries memories that long to be freed and restored. This is not just about me. This is an invitation for you as well.

Some friends told me about God and insisted that if I believed in Him, I would receive a brand-new spirit. They said this would change everything. Honestly, I thought they were out of their minds. I wanted nothing to do with a God who, in my mind, had allowed me to be abused and had handed me the life I lived. But I was wrong. As we covered earlier, God did not allow what happened to me. He did not sit passively. He was not the author of my pain or the one weaving destruction into my childhood.

If you have ever wrestled with the thought that God allowed what hurt you, I want you to take a moment to breathe this in. He did not cause your pain. He did not orchestrate what harmed you. I pray that truth begins loosening something inside you even now.

Soon after this, something shifted. I learned that God was not the only spiritual realm at work. I learned that there is an enemy who comes to steal, kill, and destroy, and that God came to give abundant life. Every horrible part of my story came from the enemy or from broken people acting from their own wounds. None of it came from God.

When that truth hit me, that same fierce, "mama bear" instinct awakened in me (as described earlier). I realized it was time for war. I had cubs now who were watching everything I did, and if abundant life was possible, then I wanted it. So I chose, for the first time in my life, to trust.

Maybe the same activation is happening in you. Maybe something in you is rising, even if quietly. Let it rise. Healing does not begin with perfection. It begins with willingness.

This brought me back to the promise in Proverbs 19:23: that when a person lives surrendered before the awe of God, they experience abundant life, continual protection, and complete satisfaction. That promise lit something inside me.

As I returned to belief, I discovered that when I put my trust in Jesus, I became a new creation. Scripture says the old things pass away and all becomes new. Some people are healed instantly and I fully believe this could happen for you even now in the name of Jesus. But for me, healing was a process—a beautiful one, but still a process.

If you are hoping for instant change, do not be discouraged if your healing unfolds step by step. God works powerfully in a moment and in a process.

Here is what I learned. My human spirit died, and my spirit was made brand new. It became pure, complete, and whole just as Jesus is. My spirit came alive. Suddenly, the connection, the communion between the Creator of the universe and me, became clearer and more alive than anything I had ever felt.

If you have never felt this, pause for a moment and simply whisper to God that you are ready. Tell him you are willing. You may be surprised by how quickly His nearness becomes real to you.

I want to tell you a testimony about a girl who never had her father around. She took a quiet moment with this same invitation. She surrendered and asked Abba to be her father. In her mind, she whispered a request no one else heard. She said If you really are my Father, then I need to feel your hand in mine the way a father holds his daughter. At that exact moment, her friend reached over and grabbed her hand. Her friend never heard her prayer. Some call these coincidences. I call them intentional encounters. Loving kindness reaching directly into a wounded place of the soul.

I share this because God is not far from you. You may feel alone as you read this, but you are not. Ask Him something secret in your heart and watch how He responds.

The next thing I learned was that my spirit had to flow through my soul before it reached my body. And at the time, my soul was filled with blockages. Trauma. Lies. Frozen places. Fragmented pieces. I needed help. And that help came from the Holy Spirit living inside me. Together, we began cleaning the wreckage. I went to a Christian counselor who could walk with me. I opened up to people who were safe and grounded in real faith. A healthy community is essential to healing.

If you feel isolated right now, I want you to hold hope. God will bring the right people into your life. Healing often begins with one brave choice to be honest.

I learned to stop living only through my five senses and instead pay attention to what was happening inside. When triggers came up, I explored them with God. Dead seeds began to be tilled out of the soil of my soul, and new seeds of life were planted and watered.

Your soil can change, too. Nothing in your story disqualifies you from healing. Not one moment of your pain is too tangled for God to unwind.

I do not know where you are in your walk with God or if you believe in Him at all. But I want to invite you into your own mama bear moment. I want to invite you to stand against the enemy who has tormented your life and partner with the Creator who fights your battles for you. If you have never let Jesus into your heart, you can right now. It does not need to be complicated. My journey began with a mustard seed of faith. I simply reached for the belief that He was good, that I was lost without Him, that I had made many destructive choices, and that He was the only one who could meet me in the torment I was drowning in.

If this is stirring something in you, acknowledge it quietly. You do not need to force it. Just be willing to let Him in.

If you are unsure, ask Him something private in your heart. Ask Him to reveal Himself. He did this for me. I was moments away from ending my life because the aftermath of abuse felt unbearable. I did not believe in Jesus because I had met too many people who talked about Him but did not reflect His heart.

In my desperation, I cried out and demanded that if He was real, He would show me who my biological father was. I had no idea at the time that he was the one who abused me. The only reason I did not end my life that night was that something in me rose up over my dog. That small spark kept me breathing. Within seven days, I found my biological father's obituary. God heard me when no one else did.

Maybe you, too, have cried out with questions that felt impossible. Maybe you have wondered if God sees you. He does. Even in the rawest places of your fear and anger, He hears.

Those years were the hardest of my life. I didn't have any of the tools I am giving you now. Maybe you feel that way too. But God was the only one who heard the cry of my soul. He answered me not by giving me the earthly father I dreamed of, but by becoming the Father my heart needed all along. He became my Abba. My Daddy. The one who guides me, comforts me, and fills the aching places where human love failed.

If connecting to God as Father feels impossible, ask Him a secret question in your heart and watch how He responds. I promise you, he will.

I will let you sit with Him now. And I will meet you in part three, where I walk you step by step through the practical ways I learned to clear the blockages in my stream, the ways I walked into real healing in my soul.

SOUL CLEANSING

Practical Tools To Detox Your Soul

You are stepping into one of the most important parts of your healing journey. Soul cleansing is where the fog begins to clear. It is where you start to understand why your reactions looked the way they did. It is where compassion begins to replace confusion. It is where God begins to show you that what felt like chaos inside you was actually your soul crying out for healing, not proof that you were broken beyond repair.

I want to continue sharing my story because testimonies

unlock courage in you. I want you to see your own story through mine and realize that the very same God who met me will meet you with the same intensity, the same nearness, and the same power.

When I began this soul detox journey, I was at rock bottom. I was finally starting to face the things my soul had been harboring for years—the same extreme physical, sexual, and verbal abuse from my own father, deaths in the family, having an addicted parent, a deeply wounded and verbally abusive stepdad, and years of poor choices that opened the door to more trauma. My soul was exhausted from decades of trying to survive. (As I described earlier in my story, these were the same wounds that underpinned my postpartum depression and the journey God led me through.)

People told me about God. They told me that if I believed in Him, I would be given a brand-new spirit that would help me. I rolled my eyes and wanted nothing to do with a God who allowed me to be abused and gave me the childhood I lived. I was convinced He abandoned me. I was wrong. As we went over in Phase 2, He did not allow those things, nor did He author them.

It was shortly after that when I learned one of the most life changing truths. God is not the only spiritual realm. There is an enemy whose full time job is to steal, kill, and destroy. God came to give abundant life. And everything horrible that happened to me was not from Him and not allowed by Him. Something rose in me that day—something wild, something protective, something like a mama grizzly bear. My cubs were watching me now. Just like those grizzly cubs who study every move their mother makes, my children were studying mine. I realized I was either going to partner with pain or partner with the God who promised abundant life, continual protection, and complete satisfaction. I decided to trust for the first time in my life.

Proverbs says that when you live a life of abandoned love and surrender before the awe of God, you will experience an abundant life, continual protection, and complete satisfaction. I held onto this with everything I had.

When I put my trust in Jesus, Scripture says I became a new creature. The old passed away, and all became new. I wish I could tell you everything healed instantly. Sometimes it does for people. Honestly, it could happen to you even right now. But for me, it was a process. What did happen instantly was this. My human spirit was reborn. My spirit was made brand new. It became perfect, mature, and complete because of Jesus. It rose. It was recreated. And that new spirit inside me became as pure as Jesus in nature. My communion with God became clearer than anything I had ever known. It was like my spiritual wifi connection suddenly had the strongest signal possible.

If you have never felt this intimacy with God, pause for a moment. Take a breath. Surrender in your heart and tell Him you are ready. He is closer than you know.

One of the first things I learned was that my spirit has to flow through my soul to reach my body. At the time, my soul was full of blockages and needed serious cleansing. The Holy Spirit, now dwelling inside me, became my Counselor, my Teacher, and my Helper. I also sought out a Christian counselor. And I told safe people who could support me. A healthy community is essential. But if you do not yet have community, I want to assure you the Holy Spirit is more than enough. You will know you are hearing Him when what you sense aligns with Scripture and the character of the Spirit of God. The Hebraic picture of the Holy Spirit (Ruach) is wind, breath, movement, life, counsel, and the one who hovers over chaos to bring order. That is what you will feel inside. Unexpected peace. Conviction that does not shame. Comfort that rises out of nowhere. Clarity that aligns with Scripture rather than contradicting it. This is how you know His voice.

And now I want to give you the practical tools that detox your soul. These are the tools that changed my life and will change yours if you let them.

STEP ONE:

Naming What Is Inside. When you surrender to the Holy Spirit, things rise to the surface because He is the best stream keeper. He is the One who moves through the soul, and nothing buried in you is hidden from Him. If the stone sealing the tomb could not stop His power, then neither can the boulders of trauma buried in your soul. So when memories come up, do not run. Trust me, I know the urge to run better than anyone. Escaping was my pattern. I always wanted to get away from the hard. Sometimes I would physically leave. Sometimes I drowned myself in distractions or work. Sometimes I numbed out with food. Sugar felt like the acceptable escape, but before I had kids, it was alcohol, sex, shopping, and stealing. My soul was a mess.

This is why Revelation 12:11 means everything to me. The word of my testimony, combined with the blood of Jesus, is the very power that brought my soul back to life. None of this healing was possible through the old version of me. Dead Sylvia could not have built a stable life or a healed heart. Only Jesus could do that, and He did it by walking into the darkest memories of my story without flinching.

As my soul was healing, memories began surfacing. Some were small and strange. Others were enormous and terrifying. One memory was buried so deep I had convinced myself it never happened. Even though I had read the court paperwork about what was done to me as a little girl, I still did not want to believe it was my biological father. That is what trauma can do. It will rewrite the story to protect you. It will build a false narrative because the truth hurts too much to hold.

But the Lord knew I was finally strong enough to face it. When my second son turned one, the memory broke open like a freight train. Not a whisper. Not slow. It came crashing in, full force. I had named my son after my biological father's side of the family. People cringe when I tell them that, but I see it now as a form of redemption. I am the daughter of the one true King, and He rewrites legacies.

I was being intimate with my husband when the memory hit. It did not whisper. It slammed into me with the weight and sound of a heavy freight train barreling forward. I had full recollection of the abuse. I could see the room. I could see myself as a very little girl. I could see my biological father. Every detail. Every sound. Every sensation. It was horrific, and it looped in my mind for over seventy-two hours without stopping. I could not sleep. I could barely breathe. And the whole time, the enemy tried whispering his lies. Why would God let this happen? Why is He letting the enemy torment you?

But a friend stopped that lie cold. She said Sylvia, God is not letting the enemy do anything to you. He is walking beside you in the valley of the shadow of death, so you can defeat this monster with Him. That truth anchored me. It shifted my whole perspective. I knew I had to face the memory, not hide from it.

I went to my counselor's office and told her I needed to do Freedom Prayer. I was terrified. Panic attacks were normal for me back then. My body would shake. My stomach would twist. I felt sick with fear. I knew she would ask me to speak in detail about the memory. The sounds. The visuals. The things that felt so disgusting they couldn't even be mentioned. I did not want to say a single word. But I knew I had to speak it out loud and call on the name of Jesus.

And when I did, Jesus Christ walked into the memory. I saw Him face to face. He looked me in the eyes and took me out of that room. In a moment, everything changed. My life is living proof of that. You cannot look into the eyes of Jesus Christ and stay the same. His love radiated colors I had never seen before. It felt like the atmosphere itself shifted.

This is not unique to me. Every woman I have stood with through Freedom Prayer has seen Jesus meet her in the place of trauma. Many of them have told me the exact same thing: He comes into the memory, He stands with them in the details, and the blockage begins to fall away. Freedom can be sudden. It can also be part of a process. Either way, do not run when your story surfaces. Name it. Speak it. Let the Spirit move the stream.

If you are ready to move into Freedom Prayer, here is a step-by-step guide that I used and teach others to use. You can find someone trained in Freedom Prayer to walk you through it, book a coaching call, or, if you feel comfortable, do it with the Holy Spirit alone. No matter which route you choose, practice safety, have a trusted person available afterwards, and follow the guidance of any medical or mental health professionals you are already working with.

FORGIVENESS

Listen. I know you may already be tired of hearing about forgiveness. Maybe every time someone brings it up, you feel your stomach tighten. I understand that feeling more than you know, not from a place above you but from someone who has walked through similar horror. None of us walks in the same shoes. Every story of abuse carries its own depth of pain, and none is greater or lesser. All abuse violates what God intended. Being abused as an infant was not acceptable. Sexual abuse beginning in my earliest months of life was not acceptable. Broken bones as a baby were not acceptable. Abuse against a child, a teenager, a woman, or a hundred-year-old saint is not acceptable. The human body was never designed to be violated. When it comes to sexual abuse specifically, God created the covenant to be a holy exchange. In Hebraic understanding, a covenant is an enacted promise cut between two people, a binding union of identity and blessing. In marriage, it is the exchange of life for life, spirit for spirit, body for body. It is not a contract. It is an intertwining. So, of course, the enemy tries to counterfeit it. Abuse is his attempt to create a false covenant, a twisted contract that tries to defile what God designed as sacred.

For years, I carried a righteous anger. I held that anger like it could protect me or keep justice alive. I believed forgiveness meant excusing what happened. Until the Lord showed me something that changed everything.

Forgiveness comes from the same root as the word fortune. The word for means in advance. The word give means to release. Forgiveness literally means to give in advance. And that is exactly what Jesus did for me—He gave in advance long before I ever knew Him. There was a time in my life when I was so hardhearted toward Him that I spit in someone's face and told them to take that to their judgment day. The coldness I walked in during those years makes me tremble now. But that is why the forgiveness of Jesus Christ became my lifeline. His forgiving nature is not sentimental. It is Hebraic. It is covenant. It means He gave Himself in advance knowing I might reject Him, knowing I might fight Him, knowing He would love me anyway.

When the Lord led me into forgiving my biological father and so many others, it came down to one posture. Surrender. I realized that nothing I held against them could change their life or mine. So I began to place myself in their defense before God. I stood as if I were their advocate, and I asked the Lord to show me their story. What happened to them as children? What shaped them? What broke them? What soul wounds were passed down that led them to become who they became?

This did not excuse anything they did. It simply positioned my heart to see them through the eyes of mercy. I brought what I knew before God with buckets of tears. For my biological father. For my mother. For my stepfather. I asked God to have mercy on their souls. And when I thought about those who had already died, I did something that may stretch some people. I told the Lord that if there was any way, any possibility unknown to me, that the truth of the gospel could reach them, then let it be so. I do not know how the mysteries of eternity work. I am not a scholar. But that posture of surrender set my heart free.

What I want you to hear is this. Do not let the enemy punk you into believing that you have not forgiven simply because you feel emotions rise again. Feeling anger, sadness, or tension when a memory surfaces does not mean you failed at forgiveness. Your soul is simply mourning. Mourning and grief are not the same.

Grief is a cycle. It creates a biochemical loop in the brain. Your limbic system is activated, releasing stress hormones. Your mind spins through sadness, then crashes, releasing another wave of emotional chemicals that pulls you back into the cycle. It repeats and repeats until you feel stuck in a fog you cannot escape.

Mourning is different. Mourning is what Scripture calls

lament. Lament is a holy outpouring. It is the act of bringing your sorrow directly to God rather than letting it cycle within you. When you lament, you interrupt the neurological cycle of grief. You speak the pain out. You name it. You hand it to God. And the brain begins to downshift. The frontal lobe comes back online. Your body begins to regulate. Your soul exhales.

Look at David. The Psalms are full of lament. He never pretended. He poured out his anguish to the Lord, and in doing so, he made space for God to comfort him. Jesus Himself lamented. He wept. He expressed sorrow without shame.

So if you have forgiven and yet emotion rises again, do not let condemnation whisper lies. Ask yourself these questions. Do you love them? Can you plead for mercy on their behalf before God? Can you intercede for their healing? If the answer is yes, then you have forgiven. What you are feeling is simply the soul mourning what it survived. Let it pour out. God meets you there.

THE WARNING AND THE WITNESS

Now I want to tell you something as a warning. Not to scare you. Not to sensationalize darkness. But because I feel responsible as your sister in Christ who has walked through these places and lived to testify to the goodness of God within them. You need to know what I have seen with my own eyes. There have been moments in my life when I found myself in rooms where deliverance was happening. I am talking about actual demonic manifestations in real people who were desperate for freedom. The first time I was in one of those rooms, I was nervous. I did not like the idea of something taking over a person's body without their permission. It felt terrifying. Deliverance scared me. Demons inside people scared me. But over time, I learned something that forever shifted the way I see spiritual warfare.

The person experiencing oppression is not powerless.

They are not helpless.

They are not victims of whatever is happening.

If they are willing, even in the smallest capacity, to take up their authority in Christ and agree with heaven, the enemy loses his grip every single time.

I will never forget this one room. People were manifesting. Teams of trained deliverance ministers were surrounding them, shouting, "Come out in the name of Jesus," but nothing was happening. And I felt so unqualified. I did not think I had anything to offer. But in those moments, God would quietly whisper something to me. I would suddenly know that the person manifesting had unforgiveness, usually toward their father.

I was never invited to help. I was not part of the team. But quietly, without drawing attention, I would kneel before the person and say, "In the name of Jesus, look into my eyes."

And then I would know exactly what to share.

I would tell them my testimony.

I would tell them what my biological father did to me.

I would tell them what happened in my childhood.

I would tell them how I forgave him and what forgiveness actually means.

Not to shock them.

Not to center myself.

But to show them what forgiveness unlocks in the soul.

And every single time, the manifestation would stop. The person would begin to sob. Tears would pour out of places they didn't know how to access. And I would gently ask them, "Can you forgive your father?" Then I would walk them through forgiveness just like I explained to you earlier.

And every time they forgave, they were delivered.

Not occasionally.

Not once in a while.

Every time.

Years later, I even received an email from one of those women. She is now helping lead women out of satanic ritual sexual abuse and into freedom. Her life became a vessel of deliverance because she discovered the power of forgiveness. Her authority was born inside the place where the enemy tried to destroy her.

After one of those sessions, a man approached me and told me he could see in the spirit. He said that in a room of hundreds, he saw no angels except two massive blue angels standing behind me everywhere I went. I do not share that to elevate myself. I share it to magnify the spiritual reality of forgiveness.

Heaven responds to forgiveness.

Darkness responds to unforgiveness.

One breaks chains.

The other tightens them.

Now I want to tell you something about my mother.

(As shared earlier, my mother watched her own father die from alcohol poisoning, never forgave him, and that trauma shaped both her life and mine. I would find her drunk in the bathroom and had to drag her out to keep her safe—these moments deeply affected me.)

For years, I thought she hated me, not realizing it was her soul manifesting the pain she never forgave. I took on drinking the same way she did because this is what happens in the soul: what we refuse to forgive, we keep, and what we keep eventually becomes the harvest we live on. I can vividly remember demons speaking to me in the bathroom. Back then, I didn't have language for anything I was encountering. Now I understand exactly what was happening.

In Hebraic thought, forgiveness means to lift, release, carry away, or give in advance. It is a word of transfer. A word of handing over. A word of repositioning something out of the soul and into the hands of God.

So if forgiveness means "to give,"

Unforgiveness means "to keep."

You keep the offense.

You keep the wound.

You keep the bitterness.

You keep the traumatic residue.

You keep what was meant to be removed.

And whatever the soul keeps, the soul eventually expresses.

This is why the enemy loves unforgiveness.

He cannot keep what you hand to God.

But he can torment what you keep inside your soul.

And here is the part that reveals God's goodness.

Today, my greatest encounters with Him happen in—of all places—the bathtub. The same room where torment once sat on me is now the very room where His presence fills me. The place where darkness whispered became the place where God thunders revelation.

This is what God does throughout Scripture.

He returns to the places where the soul was wounded and redeems them.

He met a rejected woman at a well because that is where her shame lived.

He walked into the upper room because that is where fear trapped the disciples.

He approached graves because that is where death claimed final authority.

He goes back to the place of pain and overturns it with His presence.

That is what He did for me.

And that is what He will do for you.

If there is unforgiveness in your story, do not run from it.

Do not fear it.

Do not let the enemy convince you that it is too big, too old, or too dark.

Bring it to the Lord.

Ask Him to show you what you have been keeping.

Ask Him to teach you how to release it.

Ask Him to redeem the exact place where the enemy tried to break your soul.

Because that is where you will encounter Him.

And that is where your authority will rise.

THE INVESTIGATION PHASE: TAKING INVENTORY OF YOUR SOUL

What I am inviting you to do now—for Freedom Prayer, for soul work, for real spiritual transformation—is to take inventory of your soul. This was one of the most powerful practices I ever done. It changed everything. I went back through every person who had ever hurt me and every person I had ever hurt, and I brought it all before God.

I call this the Investigation Phase.

This is where you slow down, open the drawers of your heart, and honestly examine what is still inside. The truth is this: your soul will manifest outwardly what it carries inwardly. What you do not forgive, you keep. What you keep begins to grow.

Unforgiveness is not just an emotion; it is a transaction that never got handed over. It is spiritual residue, an unpaid debt left in your soul until it collects interest in your life. Forgiveness means to give in advance. Unforgiveness means you kept it—the offense, the wound, the memory, the spiritual imprint, the bitterness, the pattern.

It is like a seed planted in the soul, and seeds grow after their own kind. This is why, when I held unforgiveness toward my mother, I didn't just carry the pain—I carried the pattern. I lived out the drinking, the self-destruction, the emotional torment I had judged in her because I had kept the transaction instead of handing it to Jesus.

In this Inventory Phase, you are identifying the seeds so God can uproot them. Here is how to walk through it:

1. The Person

Who is the object of your resentment, fear, grief, or wound?

2. The Cause

What specific action did they take that hurt you?

3. The Effect

What effect did that action have on your life, your heart, your identity?

4. The Damage

What part of your soul or instincts did that event damage? Consider your basic needs, sense of security, trust, social belonging, emotional safety, sexual boundaries, identity, and sense of worth.

5. Your Part (only where appropriate)

Abuse is never your fault. But for other situations, consider: Did I hold resentment? Did I respond in a harmful way? Did I hurt others out of my unhealed pain? Who did I affect because of what I carried?

This phase is not about shame; it is about clarity, the kind that prepares you for freedom.

Do Not Complete the Entire Investigation Phase at Once

If you are anything like me, you want to go all in. You want to fill out every sheet in one sitting, turn the process into a spiritual marathon, and be done in twenty-four hours. But the problem is this: the Investigation Phase without the Freedom Phase becomes an emotional excavation rather than a spiritual transformation. You will stir up things your soul is not ready to let go of.

Here is the rhythm I learned through experience:

- Do one person at a time.
- Immediately take that person or memory to the Freedom Phase.
- Let the Holy Spirit guide the pace.

Investigation.
Freedom.
Investigation.
Freedom.

This rhythm prevents your soul from drowning in what God wants to deliver you from. THE FREEDOM PHASE: WHERE BREAKTHROUGH HAPPENS

This is my favorite part. Some people get nervous here, but the fear is like turbulence on a plane—it feels intense, but it does not define the journey. The destination is beautiful.

In this phase, you take the memories, traumas, griefs, and wounds to God. Your soul hands them to your spirit, and your spirit places them in the hands of Jesus.

You can do this with a Christian counselor, a trusted faith-filled friend, or alone with Jesus. I have done many of mine alone with Him, and He is faithful. Before you begin, take a moment to invite the Holy Spirit and settle your heart in His presence. SOUL REDEMPTION: HANDING OVER WHAT YOU KEPT. We discussed earlier that the first part of the Freedom Prayer is always forgiveness. I am including it again here in the steps so you can remember it, return to it, and know how essential it is. Nothing changes in the soul until forgiveness is present.

I know how impossible that may feel, especially in the face of real harm. Abuse leaves marks. Trauma rearranges the soul. What was done to you was not right—no excuse, no justification. But unforgiveness will not keep you safe. It will only keep you sick.

Unforgiveness is like drinking poison and hoping it harms the one who hurt you. But it never does. It only harms you.

I have walked this path myself. I have had to forgive deep, life-shaping pain. It was difficult at first, and I know it may feel impossible for you too. Yet, what I learned through that journey—through Freedom Prayer, through wrestling with God, through giving over my soul—was that **forgiveness is not a process we can do bit by bit.**

You cannot hold unforgiveness and forgiveness at the same time. Light and darkness cannot share the same space.

This is what John was explaining when he wrote:

"God is pure light. You will never find even a trace of darkness in Him. If we claim that we share life with Him but keep walking in the realm of darkness, we are fooling ourselves and not living the truth. But if we keep living in the pure light that surrounds Him, we share unbroken fellowship with one another, and the blood of Jesus continually cleanses us from all sin."

Unbroken fellowship with Him is only accessible when we choose to forgive. That does not mean what happened wasn't wrong. It means we refuse to keep the offense or the wound in our souls.

It is righteous to hate what was done—the abuse, the verbal degradation, the neglect, the physical or emotional violence. That is darkness. That is the enemy's signature. But we are called to separate the person from the sin.

You can hate robbery, but not hate the man who robbed you. You can hate the abuse but not the abuser.

Forgiveness is not a process. Mourning is a process.

Jesus Himself said, "Blessed are those who mourn, for they shall be comforted." To grieve is to feel. To mourn is to express those feelings—to cry, weep, wail, sob, groan, lament. To squeeze out every emotion in the presence of a God who does not require you to be neatly packaged. He comforts the mess.

The Freedom Prayer Step

Once forgiveness is present, the next step is Freedom Prayer. This is where you take the painful memories, the traumas, and the grief to God. Your soul hands it to your spirit, and your spirit gives it to God.

It often helps to have a trusted friend with you, someone who also believes in Jesus and can pray with you. You can set the atmosphere with worship music, candles, or simply by going to your favorite beach or park. You bring the memory to the surface, allow yourself to feel it, and then invite Jesus into it.

If you do not have a person to sit with you, the Holy Spirit is sufficient. He is our great Counselor, our Friend, our Comforter.

He will meet you in every moment of honesty and pain.

You may remember that I previously shared my own Freedom Prayer encounter and how my father's forgiveness unlocked my soul. The story demonstrates the power of surrendering wounds to God. What I want you to take from it is this: when we bring forgiveness and memory together before God, He meets us there. He intervenes. He redeems the very place of our trauma. The story demonstrates the power of surrendering wounds to God. Identify the person who hurt you.

1. Recall the specific action that caused pain.
2. Acknowledge the effect that the action had on your life.
3. Name the damage: the ways it impacted your basic instincts, your social interactions, your sense of safety, or your emotional health.
4. Determine your part, if any. (In cases of abuse, there is none.) For other conflicts, ask yourself: How did I contribute? Whom have I hurt? How have I caused harm?

Take one person at a time. Don't rush. Combine the investigation of memories with Freedom Prayer for that memory before moving on to the next. This allows God's Spirit to begin redeeming each wound as you go.

Step Two: Mourning

Grieving is the internal experience of sorrow. Mourning is the outward expression of it. Brain science has shown that grief can distort memories and even create a chemical high when we stay stuck in it. Mourning is the antidote—it squeezes the grief out, expresses it, and releases it.

Mourning can look like wailing, crying, sobbing, groaning, or lamentation. It is a passionate expression of grief. Every dead seed in your soul—every bit of pain, trauma, and unprocessed suffering—can fall to the ground as you pour it out before Abba.

Step Three: Freedom

Once forgiveness is present and mourning has released the pain, your soul experiences the freedom that comes from letting go of what you've been holding on to. Dead seeds cannot flourish. By forgiving, by mourning, by releasing, you create fertile soil for God's restoration. You reclaim your soul and your story. You encounter God in places where trauma once had a grip, and you are restored.

TESTIMONY OF MOURNING AND RESTORATION:

My mother and I were estranged for years because of her alcoholism. She was my only biological parent, and I clung to that, never wanting to be abandoned. We were out of a relationship during the most crucial times of my life, as I was birthing children and learning to be a mother.

The pain was real and deep, likely stretching back to my time in her womb. I spent years at the beach—my sanctuary—wailing, moaning, groaning, crying, sobbing, complaining, and giving it all to Abba. In that raw, tender soil of my soul, God began to turn pain into a flourishing garden.

Three years passed before our reconciliation began. During that time, I learned to hear God's voice at the beach, to distinguish His truth from the lies I had internalized. One day, my brother called to tell me my mother was in the hospital with a brain tumor. My worst fear was losing her. Over the next three months, I navigated a storm of emotions.

When she moved back to our state, I went to see her. Abba instructed me to wash her feet. For years, her skin had been a trigger, a reminder of dragging her out of bathtubs while she was drunk and in danger. But that act became a divine encounter, a symbol of external forgiveness. Even when old offenses tried to surface during our interactions, I was able to mourn and release, and Abba comforted me.

She accepted Jesus 22 days before she went to Heaven. The Holy Spirit even guided me to record the meanings of every hospital staff member's name during her care. From start to finish, the names formed a tapestry of His faithfulness:

- Lady of God's mercy
- God of War
- God's satisfaction
- The exalted one
- Messenger of God
- From the heavens
- Universal
- Divine deliverer
- King
- Harvester
- God beholds
- Follower of Christ
- Oath of God
- God is satisfaction
- North man
- God's word
- Free man
- Graceful lily
- He beholds

- God of Earth
- Daughter of God
- Who is like God
- Woman
- Victory secure
- Living
- God of War
- Not of this world
- Loved by God
- Born again
- Pure
- Noble lighted
- Pure mother
- God has been gracious
- Fair and yielding
- Gift from God
- Wished-for child
- Worthy of love
- Shepherded

Do not be afraid to mourn with Abba. He is in every detail. Every tear, every lament, every sigh is seen and transformed into restoration. He will turn your mourning into dancing. He will bring life to the places the enemy tried to break you.

FINAL ENCOURAGEMENT

Take your time. Be gentle with yourself. Abba will never leave or forsake you. Each memory you examine, each seed you mourn, each wound you hand over, is a step toward flourishing.

You are not alone. You are not broken beyond repair. The Spirit is faithful. The soil of your soul is tilled and ready. Your freedom is waiting. I believe in you, I am here for you, and I celebrate every courageous step you take on this journey.

7

Chapter 7: Breaking the Old Roads, Building the New Ones

You have explored the deep places of your soul, identified wounds, and released bitterness and unforgiveness built up over decades. Each piece, you have handed to the Lord. Now, change begins.

When the soul is cleansed, the mind becomes ready to be rebuilt.

This chapter is about the roads your mind has traveled for years, some since childhood, and the new roads God is preparing to build. First, it explores the difference between your **mind** and your **brain**, and why Scripture speaks so consistently about the renewal of the mind, long before modern neuroscience proved how it works. Next, you will see how Hebraic thought, Greek thought, and Paul's teachings intersect with your day-to-day experience of thinking, feeling, choosing, and believing. If you are wondering how to put these truths into practice, rest assured—practical, actionable steps are coming later in the chapter to guide you through this transformation.

And it is about hope. No matter how many destructive, distorted, fearful, or shame-filled roads you once traveled, new ones can be built. I am living proof.

My friends today cannot imagine who I once was: a woman fearful of illness, dominated by trauma, seeking comfort in painful places, and convinced love had to be earned. I lived in a trap of old, painful patterns.

Those roads existed. They were well-worn. But they are gone now, replaced by paths built by the Spirit and reinforced by truth. New patterns, new instincts, new ways of thinking and responding that feel as natural to me today as the toxic ones once did.

This transformation did not happen because I became "strong." It happened because my soul was healed—and once the soul is healed, the mind can be renewed.

The Mind and the Soul: Hebraic vs. Greek Understanding

In modern Western culture, we often separate "mind," "heart," and "soul" into distinct compartments. Ancient biblical language does not divide them this way.

Hebraic Thought

In Hebrew thought, the **nephesh**—the soul—encompasses the inner life: emotions, will, thoughts, desires, and moral compass. Here, the **mind** is not an isolated processor; instead, it is part of the soul's overall activity. Hebrews understood humans as whole beings: one integrated person whose inner world exhibits itself outwardly. This contrasts with later distinctions between mind and soul.

When Proverbs says, "As a man thinks in his heart, so is he," it expresses this Hebraic idea.

The heart thinks. The soul thinks. The mind is woven through all of it.

Greek Thought

Greek thought, which much of Western culture inherited, draws clear lines between body, mind, and spirit. It highlights reason and intellectual thought as separate from emotions or the moral life, forming a distinct contrast with Hebraic views, in which the mind and soul are interwoven.

When Paul wrote to Greek-speaking audiences, he used their language but infused it with Hebraic truth. So when he spoke of "the renewing of the mind," he wasn't only talking about rational thoughts, but about the renewal of the **inner life**—the seat of choices and identity.

Why This Matters

When Scripture refers to the mind, it is not speaking of the biological brain. Instead, Scripture addresses the part of a person responsible for beliefs, habits, and interpretations—the mind, as distinct from the brain.

It refers to **the patterns, pathways, habits, beliefs, and interpretations** that grow inside the soul.

This is exactly what neuroscience now confirms.

The Brain Is Not the Mind

Your brain is an organ.

Your mind is the expression of your soul's activity, acting through your brain. The mind directs, while the brain records and encodes these directions. This distinction clarifies how healing and renewal begin in the soul and mind before affecting brain patterns. (For a deeper explanation, see "Understanding the mind's renewal" later in this chapter.)

The mind is what chooses, remembers, imagines, decides, believes, rejects, accepts, nurtures, or destroys. The brain simply encodes those choices into pathways.

When you repeat a way of thinking—fear, shame, anger, unworthiness, self-protection—your brain literally builds a pathway for it. It becomes a road, a default, a reflex—a familiar route the brain runs down automatically because the mind has sent it there thousands of times.

This is why trauma survivors can feel hijacked by reactions they don't want.

Their minds were injured, their souls wounded, and their brains built roads around those wounds. But what **the mind repeatedly thinks, the brain reinforces. What the mind renews, the brain rewires.** You are not trapped. The mind can be renewed. The brain can be rewired. The soul can heal. The Spirit can lead. With God, no pattern is too deep to change. Even the roads that feel oldest can be rebuilt with His help.

Why the Old Roads Formed

For many years, my soul carried unhealed wounds. My mother had pain rooted in her father's suicide—pain she never forgave and which influenced her later years. Her story became mine because unhealed wounds can shape the next generation.

When she drank, when she was cruel, when she was lost in her own torment, I did not understand it. I only absorbed it. I kept the offense, not because I wanted to, but because I had no language for letting it go. What we keep in the soul manifests somewhere—mentally, emotionally, spiritually, behaviorally, or relationally.

Those unhealed places in me became the blueprint for the roads I built.

Fear became a road.

Shame became a road.

Self-hatred became a road.

Hyper vigilance became a road.

Sexual brokenness became a road.

Defining myself by pain became a road.

Eventually, these roads began to feel like "who I was."

But they weren't me. They were simply byproducts of a soul that had not yet been redeemed in those places.

Renewing the Mind: Scripture Meets Neuroscience

Paul says, "Do not be conformed to this world, but be transformed by the renewing of your mind."

He does not say, "by the renewing of your brain," because transformation begins in the **mind**—the soul—long before it shows up in the physical pathways of the brain.

The Hebraic picture is of a mind made new through:
Truth
Surrender
Repentance
Worship
Identity in Christ
Agreement with the Spirit instead of the flesh
As this renewal begins, the brain follows. Old roads weaken. New ones strengthen. Soon, the new ones become familiar.

This is why I can stand today and say the Sylvia my friends know—full of conviction, trust in Jesus, purity, authority, and peace—is not a version I created through willpower. She is the result of a renewed mind and a healed soul that built new roads under the leadership of the Holy Spirit.

What Your Mind Is Capable Of

Scripture paints a far richer picture of the mind than our modern language does. The Bible shows the mind can:
It can make decisions.
It can determine a direction.
It can plan.
It can choose obedience.
It can vacillate or become double-minded.
It can be blinded or dulled.
It can remember.
It can ponder.
It can give guidance.
It can be troubled, disturbed, anxious, or doubtful.
It can be renewed, guarded, tested, filled, strengthened, or transformed.

It can be set on the flesh or set on the Spirit.

It can be shaped by the Holy Spirit.

It can carry the very mind of Christ.

When the soul is healed, and the mind is surrendered, these capacities return to their original design.

The Mind That Learns to Live Free

When I stepped into the long work of healing my soul, I did not yet understand how deeply the mind participates in that healing. I had experienced powerful moments of freedom—like when the Lord broke generational agreements in my family— but deliverance moments alone do not finish the work. They clear the soil. The daily renewing of the mind plants the new seeds.

The Hebraic worldview helps us understand this. In Scripture, the mind is not treated as a separate, cold, intellectual space. It is a vital part of the soul—thinking, feeling, remembering, imagining, and choosing. It shapes the whole person. Hebrew thought sees the mind as something that can be opened, closed, strengthened, darkened, enlightened, or transformed. It is both the seat of understanding and the center of emotional life— the spiritual center where thoughts and emotions intertwine to form the inner life.

The Bible shows this clearly. Nehemiah describes a moment where he stopped and pondered in his mind before confronting injustice—his thought life mattered to God. Paul explains that the mind can be blinded, meaning its ability to perceive truth can be spiritually obstructed. This does not refer to God Himself but to the influence of the enemy. In 2 Corinthians 4:4, the phrase "the god of this age" refers to Satan and the systems of deception that characterize the fallen world. It includes belief structures or philosophies that elevate themselves above the true God—new age spiritualities, self-divinity teachings, humanistic ideologies, and anything that promises inner light without the Lord who is Light Himself. These systems darken the mind instead of renewing it.

Jesus shows another dimension. In Mark 3, we see someone so overwhelmed, distressed, or spiritually tormented that they are described as being out of their mind. Scripture is not embarrassed to address the full range of the mind's capacity—from brilliance to confusion, from wisdom to brokenness.

As daughters of Abba, everything changes. God searches our minds to guide us. He tests our minds to strengthen them. His love can reshape troubled places. Paul explains that those who live by the Spirit set their minds on what the Spirit desires, and we can possess the mind of Christ. This is our inheritance.

As we close this section, remember: one of the most beautiful features of the mind is its ability to be made new. Romans 12:2 commands transformation through the renewing of the mind. This renewal is not optional for a believer—it is necessary for discernment, wisdom, and walking in freedom.

I remember when I first began speaking my seven-minute declarations each morning. At first, I felt nothing—but slowly, something shifted. As described earlier, patterns formed by years of trauma—shaped by my mother's drinking and the wounds I carried—began to dissolve as I forgave her and released what happened to the Lord. That was the first step. The renewing of my mind was the second.

(As explained above) Your mind and your brain are not the same. Your mind is spiritual; your brain is physical. Every time you choose to think differently, your brain physically restructures to match it. God designed your biology so that obedience to His truth creates change at the deepest levels of your body.

Research shows that most of our physical responses are shaped by the way we think. But there is no shame in Christ. If you wrestle with wandering thoughts or intrusive emotions, do not despair. The Holy Spirit is the one who reshapes the mind. Your part is agreement. His part is transformation.

If you need a place to start, try this simple prayer or affirmation:

"Holy Spirit, I agree with Your truth and invite You to renew my mind. I surrender every thought and emotion that is not from You. Transform my thinking and lead me into freedom. I trust that Your power is working in me now."

Speaking this prayer in faith can help anchor your heart to the process of renewal.

As described earlier, notice the "old roads" you have traveled—patterns like fear, shame, anger, depression, anxiety, isolation, addiction, or people-pleasing. None of these are fixed identities. They are patterns of the mind—and patterns can be renewed.

Renewing the mind always begins with a relationship with the Holy Spirit. It is not self-help. It is not grit. Renewal is something we surrender to, while also choosing intentionally. The Word of God is the Holy Spirit's instrument. Scripture describes the Word as living and active. When Paul says all Scripture is useful for teaching, convicting, correcting, and training, he is describing the Spirit's work in the mind of a believer.

So this week, begin to renew your mind intentionally. Choose one thought or one area to focus on. If you are unsure where to start, here are some common areas that many people find helpful: fear and anxiety, comparison with others, struggles with self-worth, perfectionism, people-pleasing, anger, shame, or feeling inadequate. You might notice patterns around worry about the future, harsh self-talk, or difficulty receiving love. Ask the Holy Spirit to highlight which of these resonates with you right now, or simply start with whatever feels most pressing.

I recently began asking the Lord for help in breaking old patterns of coping with food during my pregnancy. He has been showing me new things about addiction and the roots of codependency. Renewal always begins small and grows strong.

Renewing the mind is where the deep gold of transformation forms. I am proud of the courage you are carrying.

In the next section, we will move into the body and how it partners with the mind.

Four Windows into the Mind

When we evaluate our mind, it helps to look through four windows: emotions, thoughts, body reactions, and behaviors. These four areas tell you what is happening inside long before your life manifests it on the outside. Healing always begins with understanding.

1. Emotions

Emotions are signals; they are not dictators, even though for many years I let them be. I allowed people to influence my emotional atmosphere far more than the Holy Spirit did. I handed out authority to people who were not over me. That season taught me how necessary emotional boundaries are.

You may be naturally sensitive like I am. Sensitivity is not weakness; it is discernment in its raw form. It just needs to be trained. Name your emotions honestly. Identify what triggers them. Notice who consistently pulls you into reaction. Emotional mastery begins with emotional awareness.

We will talk more about boundaries and relational communication later. For now, give yourself permission to identify what you feel without apologizing for it.

2. Thoughts

Your thoughts shape the atmosphere of your life. Catch your negative thoughts the way you would catch an intruder trying to steal something precious. Ask the Holy Spirit to alert you when a thought is not from Him, and with His help, remove it and replace it.

Thoughts aligned with fear, accusation, hopelessness, or self-hatred are not neutral; they are invitations to partner with a mindset that opposes your destiny. Scripture calls these mindsets "strongholds," and they are dismantled through truth.

When financial pressure hits, when relational conflict rises, when disappointment whispers, you can choose gratitude instead of panic. Gratitude rewires the mind. Thankfulness activates peace. You cannot think fear and thankfulness in the same breath. Gratitude wins every time.

3. Body Reactions

While I do not participate in modern somatic language, I do believe the body responds to what is happening in the soul. Your physical reactions—tightness in your chest, a heavy stomach, tension in your shoulders—can reveal internal stress, fear, old memories, or unaddressed emotions. Rather than ignoring these signals, slow down and pay attention to them.

Your body often cries out before your mind catches up—not to lead you, not to define you, but to alert you.

Later chapters will give practical steps for caring for your body and partnering with the Holy Spirit to bring calm where old fear once lived.

4. Behaviors

Behaviors are the outward expression of what has been going on internally—sometimes for years. Behaviors can be healthy or destructive. Many survivors of trauma wrestle with things like overeating, restricting, pornography, impulsive sexual behavior, substance misuse, lying, manipulation, or isolation. I share these without shame because I have lived through many of them—not as isolated habits, but as survival mechanisms.

Healing does not come from condemning yourself. It comes from identifying what job the behavior is doing. Every destructive behavior is trying to meet a legitimate need in an illegitimate way.

For years, I thought I had conquered my destructive cycles the moment I lost eighty pounds and started walking in victory. But when the sexual betrayal in my marriage came to light, everything in my internal world shook. Betrayal did not just hurt; it tried to reopen the exact wounds I had overcome from childhood sexual abuse and trauma.

I gained the weight back. I spiraled emotionally. I felt crushed in places I thought were already healed. This time, instead of letting the enemy rewrite my identity through the pain, the Lord showed me I was hitting the deepest layer of the onion—the core.

Within twenty-four hours, I was shocked by a betrayal of information and lost the friend I trusted most. Everything familiar was shattered. In that breaking, I learned something far more powerful than any previous victory: my AUTHORITY. God had assigned me as a missionary to a bloodline—my own. And that bloodline bore one name: Caldwell.

What happened in my marriage, what tried to destroy me, what attempted to bury this book, has now become the very reason I write with authority. You are reading these pages on the other side of war—not theory, not detached teaching, but victory that has been lived, attacked, tested, and proven.

So hear me clearly: your behaviors are not your identity. They are indicators of where your soul still needs truth, safety, and healing—and God is faithful to meet you there.

Replacing Old Behaviors

The Holy Spirit will show you what needs to be replaced and what needs to be surrendered. He will also show you what to build in its place—whether it is truth, rest, structure, accountability, or new habits.

You can create short-term and long-term goals as you walk this out.

Example:

Short-term goal: Replace processed sugar for two weeks.

Long-term goal: Stabilize your eating habits by choosing whole foods regularly.

Remember—this is not about perfection. It is about surrender and partnership.

Practical Steps for This Week

Ask the Holy Spirit to reveal one destructive pattern you are ready to address without shame or self-hatred. Remember, God's voice is gentle and loving. You may sense His guidance as a quiet thought, a sense of peace, or a gentle nudge. Trust that He delights in leading you, and even if it feels subtle or quiet at first, you can rely on His faithfulness to guide you safely through this process.

Identify what job that behavior is doing for you.

Ask him what He wants to replace it with.

Create one short-term and one long-term goal.

Pay attention to any physical reactions you experience throughout the week and ask the Holy Spirit what they may be signaling.

He will always lead you with kindness. He will not shame you. He will not accuse you. He only sees the healed, whole version of you that Christ already paid for.

You are walking toward freedom step by step, and I am proud of you for doing the work. Phase six will take us deeper into the body and how it responds to the renewed mind.

As we close this chapter, I want to share a story that illustrates the power of the soul and the mind. In a study, children were given poison ivy but told it was harmless—almost none broke out. Another group was given harmless leaves but told they were poisonous, and many developed rashes. This shows that our soul can decide how our body will react, even before our brain interprets what is happening. The expectation, the belief, the agreement in the soul shapes the body's response.

This is why I want to leave you with one clear truth: trust the process. Every small step you take to renew your mind, redirect your thoughts, and choose truth over trauma matters. Healing is not about perfection. It is about showing up daily, tending the soil of your soul, and letting God's Spirit do the growth work.

It is normal to grieve, to feel the missing pieces of your childhood, and to remember the pain you endured. God sees every tear and is close to the brokenhearted. Your grief matters to Him; He honors it and draws near in those moments of pain. This grief does not have to trap you. It does not have to define your life. That child-version of you does not have to remain stuck in your soul. Fragmentation can be redeemed. As you tend to your soul and renew your mind, you begin to live from a place of wholeness rather than from survival.

There is a difference between thinking like a victim and stepping into action to heal. The victim mindset keeps you reactive—it looks backward, amplifies fear, makes your body tense, and your emotions chaotic. Your mind becomes a battlefield, replaying old pain, reinforcing old pathways, leaving you stuck. In contrast, the healing mindset moves forward. It recognizes trauma, grieves where necessary, and then takes intentional action to rebuild. Your body begins to calm, your nervous system can regulate, and your emotions begin to align with truth rather than lies. You become equipped to make choices that honor God and honor yourself.

Trust that every small action—choosing a new thought, replacing a negative belief, affirming a truth, forgiving, or declaring God's promises—matters. These micro steps water the soil of your soul. You do not control the harvest; God does. But you show up, and He brings the growth. I did not know how or when my healing would happen. I only knew I had to show up, and over time, I was no longer the person I had been.

Healing is possible. Growth is possible. Renewal is possible. Your soul is not stuck. The child within you does not need to remain imprisoned. God has given you the tools, the Spirit, and His Word to rebuild every pathway in your mind, every connection in your heart, and every choice you make into alignment with freedom and truth.

Take a deep breath. Step into action. Engage the Spirit. Remember the gardening metaphor: tend your soil, pull the weeds, water the seeds, and trust the harvest is coming. You are not who you were yesterday. By God's power, you will not remain who you are today.

8

Chapter 8: From Fight or Flight to Rest

Welcome to chapter eight, all about our bodies and healing in every fiber! Sisters, I am so proud of you—coming this far on your journey is an epic milestone! To celebrate, let's pause and worship together. I can't wait until one day we can all worship together in the same room, but for now, let's bless our bodies as we worship in spirit and truth. I love worship, and I love believing in my body. For a long time, I didn't trust that my body was strong or capable of protecting me. Eight months ago, I actually apologized to my body for believing the lies I had about it—and soon after, I got pregnant with my little boy, even when hormones were not aligned for conception. It was a powerful reminder of how connected our minds, souls, and bodies truly are. The health of our body actually starts in our mind. What we believe about ourselves, what we say to ourselves, and what others say to us—all of it impacts our physical bodies.

Thoughts, emotions, and fears swirling inside only stay contained for so long before they manifest outwardly.

I once read *Super Natural Childbirth*, which highlights the mind's influence on the body. One exercise has you imagine eating a lemon—and your mouth waters. This shows how thoughts of fear, stress, or doubt physically manifest if left unchecked. Ask the Holy Spirit to reveal any negative thoughts you have about your body. When these arise, counter with gratitude by naming what you love—your hair, eyes, or smile. Speak, write, and declare them daily. Writing makes thoughts tangible and starts to reshape how you relate to your body.

Body Reactions

Our bodies store sensations, feelings, colors, smells, and memories—both joyful and painful. Some memories, like the scent of the ocean, bring joy; others, like an old perfume, trigger heartbreak. Especially after trauma, our bodies hold files of past experiences. For those who have experienced sexual abuse, trauma can cause deep stress and shame. Carrying this weight can keep us in a state of fight-or-flight for years. When we moved into our lake house, the Holy Spirit whispered, *"I have brought you here to be still, to reflect like this calm water." Realizing this, I saw how long I'd run from stored pain and fear. God wanted me to rest. Rest is vital; sleep is only a byproduct. One practice I learned was a body scan: lying down, breathing deeply, noticing tension, and focusing on releasing it. As I breathed in God's peace and released stress, I slowly* cleared out my body's filing cabinet.

Healing in Every Fiber

We may reenact trauma through our bodies—skipping meals, overindulging, self-harm, substance use, or sexual behaviors. There is **no shame** in acknowledging this. Through the Holy

Spirit, we can overcome old patterns and nurture our bodies.

Sharing your story is essential. Secrets held within the limit of healing. Speaking them aloud, in safety and truth, opens the way to restoration. Your body is a vessel made to host your soul, mind, and God's Spirit. Treat it with care and gratitude. The Holy Spirit will guide you—your journey is unique. You are complete in Christ; He helps you step into fullness.

Reflection Exercise

1. Ask the Holy Spirit to reveal negative thoughts about your body.
2. Name at least three things you love about your body—say them aloud and write them down.
3. Take a slow, body-scan and notice any tension, pain, or stored stress. Breathe in peace, breathe out the stress.
4. Consider ways you may have reenacted trauma through your body. Ask the Holy Spirit to guide you in replacing those behaviors with care, nourishment, or positive routines.

Healing in your body is tied to the mind and soul.

By noticing stored files, releasing tension, and speaking truth over your body, you step into alignment with God's design and power. Every fiber of you can be restored. You've made it this far, and your journey into rest and healing has just begun. In the next phase, we will explore **the next layer of transformation— your physical wellness and how your body carries your victory.**

Coming this far is a major milestone worth celebrating. Worship honors our bodies and souls. In hard seasons, God told me to be still. At first, I didn't understand, but learned that being still is a release—letting go, surrendering control. In that place, God builds something new.

The Forms of Rest

I have been reading a book called *Sacred Rest* by Dr. Saundra Dalton-Smith, which I highly recommend. She breaks rest down into five forms: physical, mental, emotional, spiritual, and social. Each form of rest plays a unique role in our overall well-being and offers a path to renewal.

Physical Rest

Dr. Dalton-Smith says honoring physical needs shows strength. Many survivors feel pressure to push through discomfort. I used to build false armor, thinking pain meant weakness. In truth, rest brings strength. Allow your body to heal and be still.

Mental Rest

Mental rest means reclaiming thoughts and clearing your mind. As discussed in Phase 5, the mind resembles a filing cabinet. To achieve mental rest, empty the cabinet—write your thoughts, release them in prayer, and choose positive, truth-based content to nourish your thoughts.

Emotional Rest

Dr. Dalton-Smith teaches that emotions are meant to be fully experienced, not *bottled up*. Emotional rest comes from releasing performance and striving. Vulnerability leads to freedom—sharing your emotions in safety brings blessing. Remember: light and dark cannot coexist.

Spiritual Rest

Spiritual rest is where broken places mend, and you know you are deeply loved. It invites heaven's presence into your heart. Be still, trust, and let God restore you.

Social Rest

Not all relationships restore you. Social rest is creating space for supportive connections. Limit time spent on social media; research shows scrolling can feel like a crowded room. Choose refreshing interactions and prioritize those who revive you.

Rest and Eating

Romans 12:11-13 reminds us: *"Don't burn out; keep yourselves fueled and aflame. Be alert servants of Abba, cheerfully expectant."*

One area many of us struggle with is eating. Food cannot be digested properly if your body is not in a parasympathetic, restful state. I've personally wrestled with this, having lost and gained weight multiple times. For me, overeating was often a subconscious stress response—a protective mechanism.

Many women who have experienced abuse or trauma wrestle with disordered eating patterns: overeating, under eating, binge, or strict, restrictive styles.

Start a journey with the Holy Spirit to notice eating habits and self-care. Journal and seek guidance for a personalized plan.

Nurture yourself as you would a child—without shame, with

patience, and by celebrating small steps. Each step is progress.

Reflection and Practice

As we close this part evaluate your life in these areas:

1. Physical Rest – Are you honoring your body's need to pause and recover?
2. Mental Rest – Are you protecting your mind and emptying its burdens?
3. Emotional Rest – Are you allowing yourself to feel without striving?
4. Spiritual Rest – Are you being still in God's presence and trusting His love?
5. Social Rest – Are you creating space for relationships that restore you?

Dr. Dalton-Smith has a great quiz in her resources tab that can help you identify where you need rest the most.

You completed Phase Six, learning that rest is powerful and necessary for healing. Next, we'll explore restoring sexual intimacy.

Sexual Intimacy and Healing

Sexual intimacy is one of the hardest areas to navigate after sexual abuse or trauma. My journey through it was incredibly hard and confusing, and I want you to know from the start: everyone's journey is different. What worked for me may not look exactly like your path, but the principles of healing are the same. My story is a clear example of how the soul remembers, even when the conscious mind doesn't.

The abuse and trauma I experienced began when I was an infant and continued into my early toddler years. I wasn't aware of the abuse as I grew up, but the side effects were there—unseen, yet impacting every part of my life. I found myself reenacting experiences with loved ones and friends, not realizing my responses weren't normal. I even remember masturbating for the first time at age six. This became a pattern—an unhealthy coping mechanism, a form of trauma reenactment disguised as stress relief. Unhealthy sexual encounters followed me through my teenage years and early adulthood, even though I didn't fully understand why. I had been taught, through trauma, that sex equaled love. That was a dead seed planted in my heart—a seed that would take years to uproot. I was created to be loved by my Father God, yet my first exposure to sexual arousal came through abuse. As a result, I spent much of my life seeking sexual attention to feel valued and loved.

My sexuality first began to emerge when I started dating in high school. After my first heartbreak, the cycle of trauma reenactment continued for twelve years. I can remember the day I was listening to a program called *Love Line* because I was desperate to understand sex. The doctor on the show spoke about the effects of sexual abuse and how those effects can show up in relationships and marriages. As I listened, I realized—everything he was saying matched my life. That was the first time I realized I had been abused.

After this realization, I unknowingly dived deeper into alcohol and unhealthy sexual patterns. Looking back, those years were terrifying and overwhelming—but I praise God that I am still alive and now free. That girl I once was no longer exists. I have seen God face to face, and my life has been preserved. God's love, like a sunrise, rose upon me and never left. That same love is rising upon you now.

There are many different scenarios when it comes to challenges with sexual intimacy. Some may be physical, emotional, or spiritual; some may involve boundaries, trauma triggers, or PTSD responses. In the next few sections, I will cover each of these individually, offering practical guidance and encouragement. I will also speak my testimony over you, because a testimony simply means, "Do it again!" God is in the business of restoration, and He wants all His children to live fully alive and free

PTSD Triggers and Intimacy

I want to jump into one of the hardest areas for me: PTSD and the triggers that tried to invade the one place I thought was safe—my marriage.

We've already talked about the freedom I found when I prayed through my trauma, saw Jesus face to face, and experienced a deep shift in my soul.

If you experience PTSD that surfaces during intimacy with your spouse, it is important to know that you can pause and do not have to push through. Pausing is not a failure; it is a step toward safety. If parts of your marriage or intimacy feel unsafe, take a break. PTSD is not your identity, and it is not permanent. It is similar to a car alarm—your soul signaling that something foreign or harmful is trying to invade. When I first experienced PTSD, I tried to push past it, but it became overwhelming. I stopped, told my husband, and felt a mix of hopelessness and fear. Over time, I learned that God did not cause the PTSD; instead, He walked with me through it, offering comfort and presence. Seeking professional help, praying through memories, and inviting the Holy Spirit into triggers can help you regain a sense of safety and control. Healing is possible, and freedom is available.

If you need practical tools to communicate your boundaries, start with simple, honest phrases like: "I need to pause for a moment," or "I do not feel safe right now and need to stop." You can also say, "Can we check in together about how I'm feeling?" or "Let's slow down so I can feel more comfortable." Setting boundaries might look like agreeing on a word or phrase that signals when you need to pause, choosing a safe space, or establishing physical boundaries you feel comfortable with. Remember, you are allowed to advocate for your safety and healing—your voice matters in these moments.

Once you have safety and support in place, rebuilding intimacy is a gradual process. Take your time—intimacy is a sacred connection of mind, body, and soul. Communicate openly with your spouse about your pace, comfort, and boundaries. Healing is not linear, but as you move forward, God will continue to guide you toward freedom, peace, and healthy intimacy. Remember, slow and steady wins the race, and anything outside of this sacred connection is only a shadow of what God intended.

Start from the Beginning

Building a new foundation requires honesty and communication. Start by being completely open with your spouse. Although it may feel intimidating, vulnerability creates deep intimacy. A supportive partner will understand your struggles and walk alongside you.

If additional guidance is needed, consider seeking Christian counseling, recovery programs, or support groups together. Before engaging physically, take time to pray and worship as a couple. The first experiences may feel awkward, but moving through them together will strengthen your bond.

Communicate clearly about your boundaries, including how and where you like to be touched, your preferred pace, your comfort with lighting, any specific sensitivities, and any physical or sensory needs. Discuss what positions and experiences feel safe, and revisit any topics that are important to you both. Specificity in these conversations builds trust, safety, and a deeper sense of connection.

Mind, Body, and Soul

As you rebuild intimacy, remember it involves mind, body, and soul. Your mind is often running through to-do lists, worries, or memories, but you can invite the Holy Spirit to clear your thoughts and bring your soul together. PTSD memories may attempt to surface, but you can pause, visualize Jesus' presence, and allow His peace to restore you. You can stop mid-intimacy to pray, breathe, and reconnect.

This process takes patience, but the outcome is worth it. Over time, intimacy will feel comfortable, safe, and deeply fulfilling. There will be reminders and adjustments along the way—both for you and your spouse—and that's okay. The key is to communicate, pray, and move forward together.

The Power of Intimacy

Never underestimate what God designed sexual intimacy to do in a marriage. It is a weapon of unity and a fortress of love. The enemy desires division, but God's power restores connection, closeness, and passion. When your intimacy is aligned with His design, it becomes a source of joy, healing, and authority over the enemy's lies.

Ladies, this is not about perfection—it's about presence, trust, and grace. Step by step, prayer by prayer, your mind, body, and soul can heal together. The intimacy you are building is a testimony of freedom, restoration, and God's unending love. It is one of the most powerful tools in your marriage, and it is yours to embrace.

Breaking the Shame of Your Sexual Past

This is an important section. Do not rush past it. Do not skim it. If you have a sexual past that brings you embarrassment, regret, or heaviness—whether inside marriage or before marriage— this chapter is for you. Shame is a thief. It is a voice that tries to hold your identity hostage to what you once did, rather than who you have become. And nothing in your past has the authority to define your future when the Spirit of God breathes on your life.

As you know, I did not walk into marriage sexually pure. The brokenness in my soul had taken root long before I ever chose to lie with anyone. That brokenness grew into a full harvest, and I made choice after choice that harmed my own body, my sense of worth, and my soul. I remembered the encounters. I remembered the relationships. But the shame of them no longer weighs me down, because shame lost its power the moment I stepped into the true identity of Romans 8.

"Therefore, there is now no condemnation for those who are in Christ Jesus." Condemnation is the courtroom of shame. It is the voice that tells you your past holds your destiny. It whispers, "You're still that girl." But Romans 8 snaps that chain. It announces that you are under a completely different law now—the law of the Spirit of life. God does not shame His children. He covers, restores, reassigns, and transforms. He removes the garments of disgrace and wraps you in belonging. Shame breaks when identity shifts.

Here is a part of me that wishes someone had sat me down when I was younger and told me the sacredness of sexual intimacy. Not with fear, not with rules, but with truth. I wish I had understood that sex is not casual; it is covenant. Intimacy is not simply physical; it is spiritual, emotional, and soul-binding. It is like fire—beautiful and life-giving in the hearth it was made for, but damaging when carried into places that were never meant to hold it.

Let me take you back for a moment. I don't think I've shared this story yet, and if I have, bear with me—I write with five kids coming in and out of the room asking for snacks.

When I found out I was pregnant, my husband and I were not even together. My plan was to move to another country and work in professional soccer. Life took a turn I did not expect, and I ended up coming back to Washington state, where he lived. A friend from high school set me up on a coffee date with a woman from her church. Her name was Yolonda—fiery, bold, unfiltered, and deeply filled with the Spirit.

At that table, she looked straight at me and said, "Pregnant or not, if you want to follow Jesus, you should not be having sex with that man." She didn't explain the theology behind it, but something in me knew she was speaking truth. And suddenly, a memory from community college came back to me. A woman I barely knew had talked to me about soul ties. At the time, it felt random, but now I see it was a seed—one of those kingdom seeds God plants long before you ever know you'll need it.

That conversation stirred me. Seeds do that. The Spirit

breathes on them, and they wake up.

Fast-forward to telling my boyfriend that we needed to stop being intimate. I was terrified. Every fear came up, especially the fear of my child being fatherless like I was. But Hebrew thinking teaches something powerful: releasing control creates space for God to move. Control clutches. Trust opens. Control grasps for survival. Trust invites resurrection.

He responded with understanding, but he also said he didn't want to get married just because I was pregnant. That began a long process of conversations, counseling, and growth. Eventually, we married when I was nine months pregnant. God blessed our wedding day beyond anything we expected. He broke the shame over us. It wasn't instant for me—I needed a few more years for God to break shame off my sexual past before marriage—but it was all part of the healing journey that brought me to freedom.

Then there was another layer—a layer I didn't want to face. Before marriage, when my husband and I were dating, I had been unfaithful twice. I buried the secret. But when I was filled with the Holy Spirit, three years into our marriage and with two kids, it surfaced immediately. The Holy Spirit brings hidden things into the light not to punish us, but to free us. I was praying with a mentor who had walked through the exact same experience. Her testimony gave me courage. She had confessed, they healed, and they built a strong marriage. Her story became the seed that God used to prepare my heart. I came home, told my husband, and though it hurt him, he looked at me and said something that marked me forever: "I know that woman no longer exists."

That's what breaking shame does. It reveals that your past self is not your present identity. The old patterns are not who you are. The old choices are not the woman God has raised up.

And the old shame has no jurisdiction over a redeemed mind, a sanctified soul, and a Spirit-filled heart.

A part of this healing involved breaking ungodly soul ties. Many women are carrying soul ties from relationships or encounters they had before marriage—ties that still tug at their emotions, show up in triggers, or whisper confusion into their identity. Even if the relationship ended years ago, the soul connection can linger until it's broken.

If you are ready to break a soul tie, here is a simple, practical way to begin:

Step-by-step process for breaking a soul tie:

1. Acknowledge the tie. Be honest with God about any connection you feel to a person from your past.
2. Renounce the tie. In prayer, say clearly that you no longer agree with any unhealthy attachment formed outside of God's will.
3. Forgive and release. Tell God that you forgive yourself and this other person, letting go of shame, guilt, or anger connected to the relationship.
4. Invite God's healing. Ask the Holy Spirit to fill the space once occupied by this tie with His peace and presence.
5. Affirm your identity. Declare that your heart, mind, body, and spirit belong completely to Jesus.

Here's an example prayer:

"Father God, I come to You honestly and acknowledge the soul tie I have with [name or simply 'this person from my past']. I renounce any connection that is not of You, and I break agreement with everything that came from this relationship. I release and forgive them, and I choose to forgive myself. Please fill every place in my heart with Your love and healing. I declare that my soul belongs to You alone. In Jesus' name, amen."

You can pray this as many times as you need, and trust the Holy Spirit to guide you through any memories or emotions that come up.

Here are some signs you may have a soul tie:

You think of someone from your past with intensity or emotional pull.

Memories of that person interfere with your intimacy, self-worth, or marriage.

You feel guilt, shame, or confusion tied specifically to that relationship.

You dream about them or feel emotionally connected in moments of stress or loneliness.

Your body reacts (tension, fear, craving) when you think of them or replay memories.

If you are married, breaking a soul tie from before marriage does not dishonor your spouse—it actually heals your union. Your soul was designed to be entwined in covenant, not scattered among moments, mistakes, or memories.

Breaking shame frees your identity.

Breaking soul ties frees your emotions.

Breaking the silence frees your voice.

Breaking the secrecy frees your marriage.

Shame cannot survive in the presence of truth and identity. And when the Spirit breathes on your story, even the parts you wish were different, they turn into testimonies that unlock freedom in others.

Breaking Soul Ties with Your Husband from Before Marriage

Even after marriage, it's possible for soul ties to linger from before you were wed. These ties are not about your current relationship being unhealthy—they are about unfinished emotional or spiritual attachments that were created in intimacy before God's covenant of marriage. When we enter marriage carrying these ties, it can create tension, confusion, or even unspoken barriers in the union.

Scripture teaches us that a double-minded person is unstable in all their ways (James 1:8). Soul ties from before marriage can create this instability, even subconsciously. A soul that is divided, holding on to a past attachment, cannot fully rest, trust, or flow in the covenant of marriage. The heart, mind, and spirit are interconnected, so when part of our soul remains bound elsewhere, it can affect our emotional, physical, and spiritual intimacy with our spouse.

Breaking these soul ties is an act of honoring God, your husband, and yourself. It is not shameful—it is sanctifying. It releases the hold of the past and opens the door for your marriage to operate fully in God's design.

Here's what this looks like practically:

1. **Acknowledge the tie:** Confess and recognize that there is a lingering connection to a past relationship. This is not blame—it's awareness.
2. **Renounce it in God's presence:** Speak to God directly. Tell Him you are breaking the soul tie and ask Him to sever every spiritual and emotional attachment to the past.
3. **Bless your husband:** In prayer, commit your husband fully to God's care and declare that your covenant with him is

sacred, free from all previous attachments.

4. **Forgive and release yourself and others:** Let go of guilt, shame, and any lingering emotions tied to that person. Forgiveness doesn't mean excusing behavior—it means freeing your heart.

5. **Reaffirm your covenant:** Speak, write, or pray over your marriage vows again if it helps. Remind your soul, your body, and your spirit that your only soul tie is now to your husband in the sanctity of marriage.

Breaking these ties is not just symbolic—it aligns your spirit with God's design. Suddenly, your thoughts are clearer, your intimacy is deeper, and your unity with your husband is stronger. The past loses its hold, and your marriage becomes a safe, sacred space where love can flourish without hidden attachments.

Remember: God designed intimacy to be a holy union of mind, body, and soul. Nothing from the past should have a hold over what He created for you in the covenant of marriage. By breaking pre-marriage soul ties, you step fully into the freedom, peace, and joy of a marriage unshackled by old bonds.

Masturbation: A Hidden Wound, A Hidden Open Door

This is a topic most women never talk about, and honestly, that's part of the problem.

What stays hidden grows. What comes into the light can finally be healed.

For many survivors of trauma, especially sexual abuse, the habit of masturbation often begins long before they understand what is happening in their body. Sometimes it starts as the body "remembering" a stimulation it never asked for. Later, it can become a coping mechanism—because the same part of the brain involved in emotional soothing is activated through anything that releases dopamine: eating sugar, overspending, substances, exercise, or sexual stimulation.

So is masturbation "okay"?

Let's start with this truth:

There is no shame in your history.

Whether it involved fantasy, pornography, or even imagining your own husband, shame and guilt were nailed to the Cross. When you bring your past to God with honesty and repentance (which simply means turning in a new direction), you are fully covered. The Bible reassures us in 1 John 1:9, 'If we confess our sins, He is faithful and just to forgive us our sins and to cleanse us from all unrighteousness.' You are not just forgiven—you are washed clean by His love. Let this assurance comfort your heart as you walk forward.

But repentance also means **inviting God into how you live going forward**, and that's where this conversation must go deeper.

Why I don't believe masturbation is spiritually harmless

This isn't about legalism—it's about recognizing the **spiritual patterns connected to old trauma**.

For me personally, masturbation was one of the hardest areas to surrender. It felt like something I "couldn't help." But what I eventually learned was this:

The strongest urges were not my identity—they were familiar spirits trying to pull me back into trauma reenactment.

Especially when fantasy or pornography were involved, the enemy uses those moments to reopen old neural pathways of abuse, loneliness, or survival.

Even when I masturbated thinking about my husband, I eventually had to face the truth:

- I was being more stimulated by the act itself than by marital intimacy.
- I was creating an internal world disconnected from the covenant connection.
- And afterward, real intimacy often felt less fulfilling.

It wasn't a sin because the action was "dirty."

It was sin because **it divided my body and spirit**, and God designed intimacy to be **unifying**, not isolating.

Masturbation and Open Doors

When we act from wounds instead of identity, it can open doors spiritually and emotionally:

- **Tormenting urges** that feel stronger than self-control
- **Lustful thoughts** that escalate beyond what you'd normally desire
- **Shame cycles** that drain confidence
- **Disconnection** in marital intimacy
- **Dissociation** or feeling numb emotionally
- **Reactivating trauma memories** connected to early experiences

Masturbation is not "just physical." It can become a spiritual agreement—an intimacy counterfeit.

Remember:

The enemy cannot create anything. He only counterfeits what God created.

If he can get you to seek comfort, relief, or connection outside of covenant intimacy and the Holy Spirit, he will.

How to Break Free

There were moments when the urge felt so overwhelming it almost seemed like torture. But here's what I learned:

1. Interrupt the moment before the agreement forms.

You can pray out loud:

"Father, I hate this feeling. I reject this urge. I choose purity and wholeness."

2. Declare ownership of your body.

"My body belongs to the Lord and to my covenant—not to old memories."

3. Shift your attention immediately.

Open Scripture. Worship. Read a Psalm.

Distraction isn't avoidance—it's redirection of power.

4. Invite your spouse when appropriate.

Within the covenant, intimacy is healing. But this must be mutual, honoring, and Spirit-led.

5. Recognize the spiritual root, not just the physical urge.

This isn't a weakness. This is warfare.

And you are equipped.

Every time you refuse that craving, you are not "missing out."

You are **refusing to engage in intimacy with the enemy.**

No Shame—Only Freedom

We all crave things: food, admiration, escaping into shopping carts, comparison on social media—you name it. It's not that the craving makes you dirty. It means you are human and at war with your flesh.

But a woman healed by Jesus learns to recognize:

- **What is from her spirit**
- **What is from her flesh**
- **What is a familiar spirit trying to trigger old wounds?**

And she chooses victory every time.

You can do this, sister.

Not in your own strength—but in the power of the Holy Spirit who already lives inside you.

When Hunger Speaks — Understanding Eating After Trauma Moving on to Food

By the time I reached this part of my healing journey, I thought I would be writing this chapter completely from the other side— victorious, stable, fully healed, and never turning back. But I need to be honest with you, because honesty breaks shame and realness breaks chains.

During the war of getting this book out into the world, I slipped backwards. I didn't see it at first. Trauma never announces itself—it whispers. And the enemy doesn't usually shove... he nudges. During a painful season of sexual betrayal in my marriage, the enemy took an old wound from my past—one I thought was done—and reapplied pressure to it. He used stress, grief, emotions, and triggers to try to reopen the same soil he once planted in me as a child.

And for a moment, I fell for it.

I didn't realize how much the weight, the eating patterns, the old cravings, and the desire to numb myself were all part of a spiritual attack. I didn't realize my body was responding to betrayal the same way it had responded to trauma years ago. But when my eyes reopened, and the Holy Spirit exposed the scheme, I rose back up. And I am now on this same journey again, with you, not above you.

If you find yourself slipping back or repeating old patterns, please know that setbacks are part of the healing journey—they do not define you or your future. With every stumble, there is grace, and you can always start again. One gentle next step is to pause and pray, asking God for His help and clarity, or to reach out to a trusted friend, support group, or counselor. You are never alone, and forward movement is made up of small, honest steps like these.

I hope this vulnerability brings freedom, not disappointment. If you hit a bump in the road, that bump is not your identity. It's a moment, not a definition. But it *is* something to be aware of. The enemy is predictable—he uses familiar weapons. He tries to reopen old wounds. Awareness is powerful.

Now, let's talk about why eating becomes such a complex story for women who have lived through trauma.

Why Eating Becomes a Silent Battle

If you've walked through sexual abuse, betrayal, emotional trauma, abandonment, or chronic stress, your relationship with food is rarely simple. Trauma teaches the body and soul to survive in the only ways they know how. And for many women, eating becomes part of that survival story.

Here is what the Lord showed me about this part of my journey:

The Body Protects Itself From Being Seen

Many survivors are unaware that their brains learn to associate being desired with danger, being seen with risk, and being noticed with fear, prompting the body to create a protective shield that only the nervous system understands. Weight can become a form of subconscious protection—not because of weakness, but because the body remembers what the mind tries to forget. These responses are not signs of laziness, failure, or brokenness, but are simply the body's way of offering protection with the tools it has.

Food Becomes the First Safe Comfort

Trauma takes away a sense of control, and food often restores it. Unlike other aspects of life, food does not judge, demand, abandon, or violate. For those who have experienced trauma, this stability can become addictive, making food the first 'safe yes' after a lifetime of painful 'no's.' This is not a sign of weakness—it's a survival mechanism.

Trauma Changes the Nervous System

Living in a persistent state of fight, flight, freeze, or fawn can rewire the body's responses. Some people eat to calm themselves, some restrict food to feel in control, others binge to silence their thoughts, while some avoid food because everything feels overwhelming. These behaviors are not failures; they are the nervous system's way of seeking safety.

"Healthy Eating" Can Become a New Form of Control

This one shocked me the most.

Many trauma survivors jump into extreme eating styles—keto, paleo, vegan, sugar-free, fasting. None of these is wrong, and many can be wonderful. But without the Holy Spirit, they can become obsessive, punishing, all-or-nothing, or another way to silence emotions instead of heal them.

It feels like discipline, but sometimes it's distress disguised as discipline.

The Enemy Uses Eating as a Familiar Attack

Just like lust, masturbation, overspending, or emotional spirals, eating can become a familiar spirit—a repeated pathway the enemy tries to reopen, especially after betrayal, during pain, or even when you are doing meaningful work meant to set captives free. That's why your backslide wasn't a failure; it was spiritual warfare, and you got back up.

The Path to Healing

Healing is not about perfection, but about attention and awareness. Begin by noticing without judgment what triggers your cravings—whether it is stress, loneliness, fear, or resurfacing memories. Invite the Holy Spirit into these moments, asking what you are truly hungry for, what emotion is trying to communicate, and to reveal the root beneath the appetite. Remember, healing looks different for each of us; there is no formula, only personal revelation.

Be Kind to Yourself

If you had a toddler, you wouldn't punish them for wanting a donut or getting off routine. You would gently guide them, cheer for them, and comfort them.

Your soul deserves the same gentleness. You're not messy, you're human, and you're healing. Every small step forward—even after a stumble—is a victory. Your eating story is not your shame story; it's a chapter God is rewriting with tenderness, wisdom, and truth.

The Fasted Life — Feeding the Spirit, Quieting the Flesh

Fasting.

I know—bringing up fasting right after talking about eating might feel a little strange. But as I prayed over the direction of this book, I kept sensing that this chapter *had* to be here. Fasting marked some of the most transformational seasons of my life, and I believe it will do the same for many of you. So, here we are.

People often assume fasting entered my life through food, especially because at that time, I weighed around 300 pounds. Logic would say, *"Surely God told you to eat fast food first!"*

He didn't.

My very first fast was TV.

I remember hearing God speak it so clearly: *"Fast TV for 40 days."*

I thought, *TV? Really? Not sugar? Not bread?*

It made no sense to me then, but now I see exactly why He started there.

For 40 days, the only thing I allowed myself to watch was sermons. What I didn't realize was that fasting isn't primarily

about what you give up—it's about what you *make room for.*
Fasting is the act of putting down the flesh so the spirit can rise.
And my spirit didn't need another episode, storyline, drama
arc, or background noise poured into it. My soul was already
overloaded with secular input, and I had no idea how deeply it
was shaping me.

Everything we watch plants seeds—every show, every storyline, every joke.

And here's the thing I forgot to mention back in the chapter
about the mind: **your brain has only three seconds to decide
whether it will believe something or reject it**, and those decisions begin forming actual pathways inside the mind. That
means entertainment isn't neutral; it's formative.

During that fast, something broke.

Shows that used to pull at my soul suddenly lost their grip.
The junk that had been feeding my spirit quietly fell off. And in
its place, something new rose up—clarity, hunger for God, and
the beginnings of real healing.

That 40-day TV fast was the first domino in what would
become years of breakthrough. And as time went on, fasting
became one of the strongest weapons God used in my life. Even
as I'm writing this, I can feel the Holy Spirit nudging me—
there's a stronghold still lingering in my thoughts, a tormenting
cycle I haven't fully conquered. And writing this chapter is
reminding me: *It's time for another fast.*

Let me tell you about some of the strongholds fasting has
broken for me.

There was a season I battled intense hypochondriac
thoughts—tormenting fears that I would die of cancer like
my mom or grandma. It was constant and consuming. So I
went on a 40-day fast, and every single time the thought hit,

I made intentional declarations. And slowly, day by day, that stronghold broke. The fear left. The torment was silenced.

About a year ago, I did a corporate fast with women across America—three days of water only. I know people who have fasted far longer, but for me, that fast was monumental. During those three days, I listened to a book called *The Esther Mantle* by Christy Johnson—highly recommend it. She talked about the orphan spirit and how it can enter through sexual betrayal in marriage. As she listed the signs of that spirit, I felt a strange mixture of shock and recognition. Many of them weren't true of my life in general, but they *were* true in certain reactions within my marriage.

She told the listener to pause the book if anything resonated and go pray. So I did.

What happened next was not normal for me—I went into a series of visions. I watched something spiritual die. It was like God pulled back the curtain and showed me what had been operating behind the scenes.

On the third day of that fast, I walked into my kitchen, and the presence of God hit me so powerfully I fell face-first onto the floor. I couldn't move. Years ago, that idea would've terrified me. But after spending fifteen years watching other people encounter God at conferences and services—while I never did— I was overwhelmed with gratitude that God met me in *my kitchen,* of all places. That moment marked me. God responds to a hungry heart, and fasting is one of the quickest ways to feed the spirit until it overflows.

Fasting also played a major role in restoring my marriage.

If I told you I entered a season of prayer and fasting that lasted about 18 months, would you believe me? Not daily fasting, but fasting *in some form*—media, food, certain meals, social input—

constantly laying something down to fight for what mattered. Some days were beautiful. Others were downright ugly. But that season of fasting kept my flesh from filing for divorce. Truly. Fasting sustained me when my emotions wanted to quit.

During that time, I had a vision of a vow renewal in a friend's yard. Honestly, that night I told God I was done unless He showed me something different. And He did.

Fifteen long months later, that vow renewal became reality.

Fasting was the thread that held me together in the waiting.

And now, as I write this chapter alongside you, I want to share something vulnerably:

I had hoped to write about fasting from a place of complete victory. But part of the birthing process for this book exposed areas where I actually slipped backward without realizing it. The enemy tried using past sexual betrayal as a fresh attack against my identity, and for a moment, I fell for the lie.

But my eyes are open again.

I'm back on the journey.

And I hope my honesty helps someone else. A bump in the road isn't failure—it's an invitation to wake up, re calibrate, and refuse the enemy's tricks.

We fast because our flesh needs reminders.

We fast because our spirit needs strength.

We fast because deliverance isn't always a moment—sometimes it's a lifestyle.

And fasting, my friend, is one of the most powerful tools of victory God has placed in our hands.

The Invitation to Fast — A Doorway Into Breakthrough

So I have to ask you honestly: after hearing my stories, are you intrigued by fasting or a little scared of it? Most women feel both at the same time. Fasting has this mysterious weight to it, almost like it's reserved for someone holier or stronger or more disciplined than the average believer. But I want to show you that fasting is far simpler—and far more beautiful—than the way it's often portrayed. It isn't a mountain only the spiritually elite climb; it's a doorway God extends to ordinary women who want extraordinary freedom.

Let's slow down together and look at fasting through the eyes of Scripture, especially through the Hebraic mindset that Jesus Himself lived and taught in. When you understand fasting from that perspective, it no longer feels intimidating. It starts to feel like an invitation.

The Hebraic Picture of Fasting

In Hebrew thought, fasting is not about punishing yourself or proving you're spiritual. It's not about starvation. The picture is much simpler: fasting is closing one door in order to open another. It is the intentional lowering of the flesh so the spirit can rise and hear clearly.

There is a Hebrew idea embedded in the word for fasting—*tsom*—that points to withholding for the sake of alignment. It is a humbling of the soul, but not in a harmful way. It is more like turning down the volume on your own desires so you can hear God's whisper again.

In the Hebraic perspective, fasting is simply about making space—not earning, proving, or punishing, but intentionally creating room for spiritual clarity and connection.

The moment you grasp that, fasting stops feeling like loss and starts feeling like an invitation. You are not depriving yourself; you are awakening yourself. You are closing the mouth of your flesh so the mouth of your spirit can speak again.

Fasting in Scripture — Breakthrough by Design

If you walk through the Bible slowly enough, you begin to notice something woven through the stories of deliverance, calling, and breakthrough: fasting appears again and again, always at turning points, always in moments where heaven presses into earth.

A single day of fasting in Israel often marked repentance, a holy reset of the heart.

Three days, like Esther's, were used to reverse decrees of death and release divine protection.

Seven days represented a completion of cleansing or transition.

Daniel's twenty-one days brought revelation and angelic assistance that had been delayed in spiritual warfare.

And the forty-day fast—seen with Moses, Elijah, and Jesus—was connected to identity, calling, and major strongholds being broken.

You'll notice something: the length of the fast always matched the depth of the breakthrough needed. Scripture never treats fasting like a formula. It treats it like a partnership. God responds to humility, not numbers. But the pattern shows us that fasting has always been one of the most powerful spiritual tools God gives His people when they need clarity, deliverance, or transformation.

So What Actually Is Fasting?

If I had to describe it as simply as possible, I would say this:

Fasting is giving up something natural in order to receive something spiritual.

That's it.

Fasting is not only about food. Sometimes the thing God asks you to fast is the thing clouding your spirit. That's why He asked me, at 300 pounds, to fast from television before He ever asked me to fast from food. He knew that my spirit didn't need more entertainment; it needed space, silence, and truth.

When you fast, you are not proving yourself holy. You are clearing out the noise so you can hear the Holy One.

Starting With Simplicity

The most common mistake people make is assuming fasting must be extreme to be effective. But the truth is that fasting is powerful because of its direction, not its difficulty.

If you are new to fasting, you can start small. Consider skipping a meal, giving up social media for a few days, or turning off the TV for a month. You might also try taking a break from certain types of music, stepping away from online shopping, putting aside your favorite podcasts, or giving up an activity like video games or caffeine. You could even fast from using your phone in the evenings, or choose a day to spend in silence without background noise. Everyone's fast is personal—choose something that you notice fills your mind, time, or energy. What matters is not what you remove but what you make room for. Fasting is never just about absence; it is always about exchange. If you remove food but don't feast on Scripture, you only succeed in being hungry. But if you remove something and fill that space with prayer, reflection, or simply an open heart before God, it becomes holy ground.

Expect fasting to expose things, bring emotions to the surface, uncover old lies, bring resistance, and create moments when your flesh complains. These experiences are not signs of failure, but indicators that the fast is working.

And above all, expect grace. Fasting is not pass or fail. It is a spiritual posture, not a test. If you stumble, you simply stand up and continue. God responds to the heart, not the perfection.

Why Fasting Works

Fasting works because it does something internally that nothing else quite touches. It silences the flesh so the spirit can strengthen. It uncovers hidden beliefs and unhealed places. It detoxes not only the body but the mind. It unclutters the soul. It reposition your attention toward God instead of toward fear, distraction, or self-reliance.

Think of fasting like cleaning a closet. Nothing new can fit until you remove what's crowding the space. The process might feel messy at first—things pulled out, memories unearthed, emotions stirred—but it is all part of making room for something better.

Fasting isn't the suffering of the body.

Fasting is the awakening of the spirit.

A Closing Invitation

Fasting is not about perfection; it's an invitation for anyone seeking clarity, healing, a breakthrough, or a deeper connection with God. It is a sacred exchange—a re-calibration, a weapon for spiritual growth, a path toward freedom, and a doorway into greater intimacy with God. This opportunity is available to everyone.

9

Chapter 9: The Rise Into Your New Life

Starting a healed life takes more than just inner restoration; it means learning how to communicate and set boundaries. It might sound simple, but trust me, this part can be really tough. It was for me, and sometimes still is. I would have gladly paid for the clear, spiritual, and practical guidance I'm about to share with you. Ahead, you'll find not only encouragement but also practical steps and exercises you can use right now. If healing your soul feels like digging deep, this part is like building a new home on the land you've reclaimed.

The number one thing that keeps people from communicating honestly, kindly, and with clear boundaries is fear—specifically, **the fear of man**, especially when the "man" is someone close to us.

Scripture is blunt about this:

"For am I now seeking the approval of man, or of God? ... If I were still trying to please man, I would not be a servant of Christ."

—Galatians 1:10

We were never called to serve people's reactions. We were

called to serve God.

Here's where it gets messy: sometimes, before a big change happens, there has to be an eruption underneath. Growth can shake up what's unstable before it brings stability. But like the Hawaiian islands, these eruptions don't just cause destruction—they create new land, new beauty, and new space that people want to visit.

You aren't responsible for moving other people's mountains or preventing their eruptions. Instead, focus on cultivating your own beautiful island—your own resort. Communication and boundaries are key as you step into your promised land.

As you worship, ask the Holy Spirit to show you if you've put anyone on a pedestal—anyone whose opinions you've valued more than God's. Be brave and ask Him to reveal where you've been afraid to speak honestly, and to help you see any lies, pressure, or expectations from others that have influenced your choices. Use what you learn as steps toward your freedom.

As you rise into your original design, people-pleasing will feel unfamiliar. The tension between your old performance and your true self intensifies. This is not failure, but growth—a detox of your identity by the Holy Spirit.

So let's talk about what actually drives these patterns.

The Root: Codependency and the Fear of Man

Fear of man is a form of misplaced trust.

"The fear of man lays a snare, but whoever trusts in the Lord is safe."
—Proverbs 29:25

When we live in fear of people's reactions, we hand them the authority God never asked us to give away. Codependency is not love—it's bondage disguised as loyalty. And most of the time, we learned it in childhood. It was normalized. It was rewarded. It felt like survival.

But now you are learning a new way.

Here's a simple exercise:

Think of all your relationships—every friend, family member, mentor, coworker. Now identify the ones that are life-giving. The ones that feel safe. The ones that don't drain you. If you find you don't have any like that, it's okay. Truly. The Holy Spirit becomes that safe relationship for you first.

Now go deeper. Ask yourself:

- Do these relationships offer mutual respect?
- Do we listen to each other?
- Do we forgive each other?
- Can we disagree and still remain connected?
- Do we feel safe with one another?

Then consider the relationships that feel hard. Ask the same questions, but add these:

- Do they hurt me physically or emotionally?
- Do they try to meet needs, or only take?
- Am I safe?

If the answer is *no*, and you are in a physically or emotionally unsafe environment, please contact a crisis line or safety center immediately. I've placed resources in your resource tab for this.

Once you've evaluated your relationships, hear this clearly:

Don't fall into trauma reenactment by seeking relationships that recreate your childhood patterns.

There is **no shame**. Your brain learned survival. Your caregivers' brains were shaped by their wounds. Now you have knowledge and can apply it. Application becomes wisdom; wisdom, freedom; and freedom, a new history for your family line.

You do not have to stay powerless.

You do not have to stay hopeful while being hurt.

You do not have to stay believing "maybe this time will be different," only to be disappointed again.

You get to choose healthy relationships. If that feels new, start small: dream and imagine it. Visualization isn't wishful thinking—imagining healthy connections helps your brain change old habits and build new hopes. Even if you feel stuck, picturing positive change can help you move from survival to hope. Try making a Pinterest board of what healthy connections look like to get started.

So What Do You Do With the Hard Relationships?

First—**pray**. Ask the Holy Spirit for a plan—for your heart and theirs. Become aware of your emotional and physical boundaries. Remember: forgiveness is not trust, continued access, or agreement. It is your key to freedom. You don't have to stay in a relationship or allow the same patterns to repeat. But you get to forgive, bless your enemies, and pour out the raw, unfiltered emotions before Abba, mourning the loss of what you hoped someone would be. Every time you do, you come out lighter, you come out dancing.

Understanding Emotional Boundaries

God made you with emotions, and that's not just okay—it's sacred. Emotions are signals, not rulers. They show what's in your heart but shouldn't control your life or relationships. Healthy emotional boundaries sound like this: "I feel sad," not "You make me sad." "I feel anxious," not "You give me anxiety." "I feel angry," not "You made me this way." For years, I gave my emotions to my husband like they belonged to him. When he was loving, I felt great. When he was distant, I fell apart. My feelings depended on his actions. That wasn't love; it was codependency. And it wasn't just with him—it showed up in friendships, family, work, and childhood. I thought everyone's feelings were my job, and mine were theirs. We learn these patterns like a language— we watch, absorb, and live them. But now, your inner language is changing. And yes, change is uncomfortable. Yes, volcanoes erupt. Yes, lava flows.

But hear me: the lava monster is as fake now as when you played "the floor is lava" as a kid. Places burned by lava become fertile ground for growth, healing, and legacy.

Instead of saying, "*You make me feel*," try using I-statements—simple changes that make a big difference. Say things like, I want to..., *I will do this by..., I might need support...*, *I feel..., I am...* This small shift is actually very biblical. Jesus shows us in Matthew how to handle conflict: go to the person first, speak truth with love, seek reconciliation, and keep your heart pure before God. Boundaries aren't rebellion; they're a sacred way to care for your heart, peace, and relationships.

From my experience, family is often the hardest place to set new boundaries and change how you communicate. Generational patterns can make your growth feel threatening or offensive to others, even though your goal is healing and freedom. Your change shines light into darkness, and the enemy can use offense or persecution to discourage you. This part is tough, but necessary.

I spent many hours tucked away in my hidden place with God, expressing every emotion I had, mourning, asking Him to help because my heart felt so deeply hurt. And every single time, He showed up. Often, He would meet me with a rhema word or a prophetic promise that carried me through the next season. These weren't just "nice thoughts"—they were lifelines. They kept me from turning around, going back to Egypt, and abandoning my promised land.

I still remember what He spoke over me—the promise that my mom would come back to me as Joseph's brothers returned to him. I clung to that promise through persecution and misunderstanding. Even when fear or offense threatened, God's presence protected me, and it will protect you too. Your heart may ache, but as you mourn and receive comfort, you are renewing old pathways in your brain that were once addicted to grief, fear, and loneliness.

Remember the Scripture:

"When you live a life of abandoned love, surrendered before the awe of God, here's what you'll experience:

Abundant life.

Continual protection.

Complete satisfaction."

—Proverbs 19:23

As you consider your family, take decisive action: write a brief outsider's perspective of your family, then clearly identify and dispel the myths you notice.

From the outside, my family looked complete—almost picture-perfect. A mom and stepdad, though most people never knew he wasn't my biological father. Steady jobs, married for twenty-three years, three kids who played sports, worked, and excelled. Camping trips, vacations, a home with dogs, and a beautiful yard. A mom who worked nonstop to provide for us. If you had asked me years ago, I truly would have said my family life was amazing. And there *were* beautiful things in it.

But when my healing journey began, I awakened to see the toxic environment beneath the surface. Alcoholism had been normalized. Codependency was labeled as passion and loyalty. Fear of death was disguised as protection and responsibility. Poverty mentality pretended to be humility. Connection only existed in chaos. No one talked unless there was a crisis, and holidays were hosted with alcohol as the main guest.

These were things that needed to be exposed to the light. They were darkness masquerading as normal. And being the one to expose them—the lone ranger—does not come without a battle.

As you start to bring things to light—through your new path, your words, or Spirit-led talks—it's important to let go of blame. Jesus has already carried your shame and guilt. He invites you to accept what happened without letting it shape who you're becoming.

So pause. Go back to your dream board. Remember your why. That is the destination these boundaries are leading you toward—the place of peace, grounded identity, and generational transformation. You can do this, friend.

Now you might wonder: *How do I actually communicate new boundaries?*

A simple place to begin is this:

First, define what you need. Identify the boundary.

Then communicate it. Speak it clearly, kindly, and simply.

Keep your words simple. Don't over explain—this was a big challenge for me. The codependent part of me wanted to explain everything to protect others' feelings. But being simple is actually stronger.

And finally, set consequences—share why the boundary matters and what will happen if it isn't honored. Not as punishment, but as protection for your peace and the calling God is shaping in you.

Boundaries are not walls; they are gates. They don't push people out; they invite healthy connections in. Instead of managing relationships out of fear, you are cultivating the sacred land of your heart with wisdom, truth, and the safety of God's presence.

When Boundaries Become Freedom

For most of my life, the word **boundaries** felt like a threat. A limit. A cage. Something other people needed, but not me. I thought boundaries meant punishment, restriction, and hearing "no" in a way that made me want to rebel. If someone said, *"You can't have that,"* my brain would say, *"Watch me."* Especially when it came to food.

Food was my comfort, my reward, my stress relief, my escape, and, honestly, sometimes my best friend. On top of that, I lived for spontaneity—*What sounds good right now?* Seven meals later, I still didn't know what I truly wanted; I only knew I felt guilty, tired, inflamed, discouraged, and confused.

Then one day, I stumbled onto something that truly changed everything:

Boundaries from God are not restrictions; they are protection, clarity, and freedom.

The verse that unlocked everything for me was:

"The boundary lines have fallen for me in pleasant places; surely I have a delightful inheritance."
—Psalm 16:6

For years, I read that verse and thought, *Pleasant places? Boundaries? How?*

Those two words never belonged in the same sentence for me.

But as the Lord started healing my relationship with food, something beautiful happened.

My Testimony: The Moment Everything Shifted

Recently, I reached a point where my eating felt completely chaotic. I was tired of fighting with myself over every decision— every meal, every craving, every "should I or shouldn't I." My willpower felt used up by 9 a.m. And then I learned the science behind why.

Your brain is not designed to make hundreds of food decisions a day.

Every choice uses up your mental energy. This is called **decision fatigue**. When you add emotional triggers and stress, your brain looks for the fastest dopamine hit—usually sugar, flour, or processed foods. It wasn't about being weak. My brain was just tired. When I learned this, it clicked: **I didn't need more willpower. I needed boundaries. Godly boundaries. Pleasant boundaries.**

So I started implementing simple food boundaries—clear, predictable, loving, *protective* boundaries.

And the pressure that lifted off my shoulders was unbelievable. I didn't have to stand in the kitchen negotiating with myself every five minutes. I didn't have to fight cravings all day. I didn't have to wonder if I was doing "good enough."

I just followed the pleasant boundaries that brought peace instead of chaos. For the first time in forever, **I began to lose weight without losing my mind.** I wasn't fighting myself anymore. I wasn't swinging between restriction and rebellion. I wasn't guilt-eating or shame-spiraling. I was free.

Why These Boundaries Work: A Quick Look Inside the Brain

This freedom isn't magic—it's biological.

When it comes to food:

- **Dopamine spikes** from sugar/flour mimic addictive cycles.
- **Willpower is finite**—research shows it depletes like a battery.
- **Decision fatigue** leads to impulsive choices.
- **Brain chemistry loves predictability.**
- **Boundaries reduce stress signals** and increase calmness.

What looks like "restriction" on the outside is actually **a relief** inside. Your body likes knowing what to expect. That's why godly boundaries feel very different from worldly restrictions: Restrictions say, *"Stay small."* Boundaries say, *"Stay safe."* Restrictions punish. Boundaries protect. Restrictions drain you. Boundaries give you back your energy. When God says, "The boundary lines have fallen for you in pleasant places," He means:

These limits bless you. These limits free you. These limits lead you to your inheritance—not away from it.

As the Holy Spirit taught me about food boundaries, I realized: Boundaries apply to every area of life.

If someone pressures you to eat something that doesn't align with your plan—boundaries protect your health. If someone pressures you to buy something you can't afford—boundaries protect your finances. Boundaries aren't selfish; they're stewardship. Any area where chaos, guilt, anxiety, or confusion shows up is usually an area where boundaries need to be established.

Physical Boundaries: Rebuilding What Trauma Broke

Physical boundaries are a whole different layer—and they are **super cool** once you understand them.

When someone has experienced sexual or physical abuse, the body's natural sense of safety gets disrupted. Your perception of "too close," "too loud," "too much," or "not safe" gets mixed up with survival responses and trauma memories.

I remember taking a class on sexual trauma and doing an exercise that completely changed how I saw physical boundaries. I want to walk you through it.

Physical Boundary Exercise

Close your eyes.

Tune into your environment.

- What feels comfortable?
- What feels uncomfortable?
- What do you hear?
- What do you smell?
- Is the temperature cozy or irritating?

Open your eyes and write down everything you notice.

Then go through this list and pay attention to what your body says "yes" to and what it says "no" to:

- An amusement park
- A plane
- A quiet room
- A day on the beach
- A city bus
- A long walk down a country road
- A small room
- A dark coffee shop
- An escalator
- An elevator
- A large room
- A crowded sidewalk
- Somewhere with no exit
- Holding a baby
- A room full of kids
- A room full of adults
- A party
- A dock on a lake
- Hugging someone

As you reflect, ask the Holy Spirit to highlight patterns.

Discovering Your Physical Boundary Normal

This exercise shows you what your body experiences as safe or unsafe. There is **no shame** in any of it. Sometimes the discomfort is an irrational fear. Sometimes it's unresolved trauma. Sometimes it's wisdom. Sometimes it's your body saying no long before your mouth does. I want to share a personal example.

My Narrows Bridge Story

For a long time, I was terrified of driving over the Narrows Bridge—similar to the Golden Gate Bridge in the PNW. Every time I thought about it, I pictured myself passing out, crashing, or drowning. Completely irrational, right, or so I thought. As God healed layers of trauma, I learned something heartbreaking. My biological father had once threatened that if I ever told anyone what he did to me, he would push my mom and grandma off that exact bridge. My body remembered the threat even when my mind didn't. That fear wasn't irrational. It was protective. My body was trying to create a physical boundary. With healing came courage, and eventually the Lord used that bridge to lead me into a major season of freedom. This is why we must ask the Holy Spirit: **Is this fear irrational—or is it connected to healing?** Once you know which one it is, you can build healthy physical boundaries around it.

My Personal Physical Boundaries

One physical boundary I have is never driving **alone with a man who isn't my husband**, even close friends. I also don't meet with men alone. Not because I'm afraid, but because I'm wise. It protects me, my husband, and our marriage. Wisdom isn't weakness; it's worship. Another boundary I keep is not forcing **myself to go anywhere I feel physically unsafe or emotionally mistreated.** If a family gathering means verbal attacks or shaming, I don't go. And that's okay.

My husband and I went through a very long season of spiritual and emotional warfare, including sexual betrayal through pornography, repeated lying, and frequent emotional outbursts from us both, and me succumbing to rage. I was completely devastated, confused, and alone in a brand-new state where we didn't know anyone. I had no family nearby to lean on, but I had God. My mind was constantly under siege, and I was angry at the enemy—here I was, building a life to help women find freedom from sexual sin rooted in abuse and trauma, and my own family was disrupted like a grenade going off.

Both my husband and I were dealing with deep trauma responses, and I often wished he had set firm, healthy boundaries when I was reacting with intense anger. It took a while before I was calm enough to really listen to God, but he encouraged us to turn to **Matthew**. It felt like we were put in time-outs, left to work things out on our own—but it wasn't really a punishment. What we found in Matthew became one of the greatest gifts to our lives, our legacy, and to each other:

Biblical Boundaries from Matthew

The scripture gave us a clear guide for handling conflict and protecting our hearts:

1. **Address sin privately first.** Speak directly to the person who has wronged you before involving anyone else (Matthew 18:15).
2. **Bring witnesses if necessary.** If the issue isn't resolved privately, bring one or two trustworthy witnesses to help clarify the situation (Matthew 18:16).
3. **Involve the church or community if needed.** If the person still refuses to listen, take it to the larger spiritual community for guidance and accountability (Matthew 18:17).
4. **Set relational boundaries if unrepentant.** If there is still no reconciliation, protect your heart by limiting interaction

until there is genuine repentance (Matthew 18:17b).

After about a year of prayer, I realized that our situation could be handled through these biblical boundaries. We had to practice them consistently—and we also had to practice **no physical boundaries** for a season, learning to slow down, reset, and protect our hearts. Here's what helped us—and honestly, it's valuable for anyone to learn at any age:

Physical Boundaries in Dating & Marriage

1. **Only date someone who shares your standards.** Someone who merely "tolerates" your boundaries will eventually lead you to compromise them. Find someone who honors God enough to honor you.
2. **Talk about boundaries ahead of time.** The moment of temptation is not the moment to decide. Decisions made in the light are betrayed in the dark.
3. **Ask a better question.** Don't ask, "How far is too far?" Instead, ask, "How can we honor God with our bodies?" It changes everything.
4. **Talk with other, older couples.** Wisdom is contagious— borrow it generously.
5. **Don't do everything at once.** Physical relationships build over time. Take it slow. Your future self will thank you.
6. **Keep your physical and emotional seriousness aligned.** If you're not emotionally committed, don't behave as if you are physically committed. Misalignment leads to heartbreak.
7. **Plan ahead and flee temptation.** This isn't legalism; it's wisdom. Jesus told us to run from sin, not flirt with it.

Boundaries Are Pathways, Not Walls

Friend, boundaries are not about restriction—they're about freedom. They help you return to yourself. They help you:

- Hear God more clearly.
- Calm your nervous system.
- Heal your body
- Rest your mind
- Strengthen your relationships

Boundaries are where true freedom grows—whether with food, finances, relationships, or personal safety.

If you have questions or need support, feel free to reach out anytime at **livecalledwell@gmail.com** or message us on social media. You are not alone. You are growing. You are healing. And your boundary lines—yes, your boundary lines—are falling in the most life-giving places.

10

Chapter 10: The Craving Within

I felt strongly that this chapter belonged here, even though it wasn't planned. My priority is to ensure that only what God wants appears in this book.

I want to discuss The Craving Within with you.

My story is what many would call addiction. I'll never forget attending Celebrate Recovery, where I was encouraged to introduce myself as an addict. Instead, I chose to say, "Hi, my name is Sylvia, and I am a Jesus girl overcoming _____." If you struggle with labels like "addict," know you can speak the truth of who God says you are, not what the world calls you. Scripture reminds us: "If anyone is in Christ, he is a new creation; the old has gone, the new is here!" (2 Corinthians 5:17). Here are some affirmations to declare your real identity:

- "I am a child of God, bought with a price." (1 Corinthians 6:20)
- "I am more than a conqueror through Him who loves me." (Romans 8:37)
- "I am set free by the Son and free indeed." (John 8:36)

- "I am being renewed day by day." (2 Corinthians 4:16)
- "God is working all things together for my good." (Romans 8:28)

Speak these truths over yourself daily. Let God's Word replace old labels with your real identity.

Before we dive deeper, let's look at where the word addiction comes from. It originates from the Latin addictus, meaning "given over" or "bound" to something. In Roman times, it referred to someone who had been surrendered to a creditor as part of a legal obligation. Over the centuries, it became the term we use for being enslaved to habits, substances, or patterns.

God didn't design us to be bound like that. He gave us cravings for Himself. In Hebrew, t'shuqah means deep longing or desire. Our hearts—lev—are made to yearn for fulfillment, and only His presence can satisfy. Psalm 42:1-2 says, "As the deer pants for streams of water, so my soul pants for you, my God. My soul thirsts for God, for the living God." This is not just poetry—it's your soul's design.

The world's labels—addict, alcoholic, broken—keep you from embracing your God-given identity. Clinging to these labels ties you to past mistakes and goes against God's design. You are not defined by yesterday.

Our souls crave God, but when we don't choose Him, we reach for substitutes. That's when patterns, habits, and compulsions take root—not from irreparable brokenness, but because we're made for more and seek the wrong thing. When we turn to God, the craving becomes life-giving. Romans 8:14-15 reminds us: "For those who are led by the Spirit of God are the children of God... and you have received the Spirit of adoption as sons, by whom we cry, 'Abba! Father!'"

Your craving isn't a weakness—it shows your soul was made for God. When you turn your craving toward Him, you're no longer bound by your past.

Now, it's important to understand why so many women struggle with what the world calls addiction. Studies show that nearly all women who struggle with alcoholism have histories of sexual abuse. This isn't a coincidence. When the soul is violated—boundaries crossed, trust broken, intimacy taken— the heart reacts. It panics. It screams for comfort. It clutches anything, anyone, or any habit that promises even a glimpse of relief. If this is part of your story, please know you are not alone and there is hope for healing. Gently consider taking a next step like reaching out to a trusted counselor, joining a support group, or inviting someone to pray with you. Healing often begins with allowing yourself to be seen and supported.

Addictions, compulsions, and harmful habits are desperate attempts to find comfort, safety, or control—but they never fill the emptiness inside. Alcohol, food, pornography, or overworking may numb pain, but only God truly satisfies the longing in your soul. Everything else is a temporary substitute that leaves you emptier.

Let's address an assumption that may arise: some people think addiction runs in bloodlines, and that you are "destined" to follow your parents or grandparents. This isn't true. What often passes through generations are word curses, mindsets, and patterns of broken thinking—not DNA. Generational pain and trauma create fertile ground for craving something to fill the soul, but the root issue is spiritual, not biological. God's Word is full of stories where broken cycles shatter when the Spirit steps in. Exodus 20:5-6 shows God's heart: the consequences of sin can extend, but His mercy is greater for those who turn to Him.

A violated or misled soul will reach for comfort. But when God's Spirit is invited in and the soul learns to cry to Him, real healing starts from within. Addictions cannot meet the soul's needs, but God can. Your longing that once led to destructive patterns becomes a divine invitation: a chance to live free and full as He intended.

Your craving isn't shameful—it's your soul calling you home. But home isn't substances or temporary fixes; it's God's presence. The craving within acts as a compass, pointing you to your Creator. When you feed it to Him, every misplaced craving loses its power, and your real identity comes alive.

To close this section, I'll share a personal moment. I will never forget the day I was going to grab a piece of chocolate—sugar-free, sweetened with stevia—and the Holy Spirit spoke to me so clearly: "Sylvia, a spirit of addiction doesn't pick what it's addicted to."

That moment made me examine my boundaries and intentionally choose what to protect. I decided to refrain from sugar, flour, and coffee—not for vanity or perfection, but because I once used them to fill my soul. Even things that seem harmless can become substitutes for God.

I started noticing how I felt after drinking coffee. Suddenly, it was like a "joy pill" in my hand. I wanted more. Honestly, it reminded me of the first buzz I ever had after drinking alcohol. And if I justified it because I was tired, it made me ask: what was out of whack in my body, my schedule, or my striving that made me feel I needed a substance to keep going?

I don't call myself a coffee addict or say I am an alcoholic in recovery. Instead, I recognize the conviction from the Holy Spirit. I need to put on my new clothes, choose differently, and refrain. 1 Corinthians 6:12 says, "All things are lawful for me," but Paul reminds us, "but not all things are helpful. All things are lawful for me, but I will not be dominated by anything." That verse is powerful for anyone walking in freedom. Not everything you could do is good for your soul. You do not have to be dominated by anything—substance, habit, or craving included.

Recognize where you need help. I didn't overcome my habits alone—I prayed, sought accountability, and surrendered pride. God often uses people to bring healing and support. Accountability can look like reaching out to a friend, joining a church group, or inviting a mentor to walk with you. Freedom comes from admitting need and letting the Holy Spirit break strongholds.

Some signs that pride, not surrender, is in control:

- Justifying indulgence because of tiredness, stress, or emotions.
- Minimizing the impact of a habit or substance on your spiritual, emotional, or physical life.
- Comparing your struggles to others and feeling "better than" them to avoid admitting a need for help.
- Repeatedly saying "I can handle it" instead of asking God or others for guidance.

Self-sabotage often stems from trying to prove independence rather than embracing dependence on God. The truth is, our souls were created to crave Him. When we attempt to fill that craving elsewhere, no habit, substance, or behavior will ever truly satisfy. But when we invite Him, embrace accountability, and surrender in humility, strongholds fall, cravings redirect, and freedom becomes real—it's no longer theoretical.

Now I sit here, 12 years past my last drink, and I will never forget what a counselor once told me. She drew a timeline and said that every substance has a tipping point. She drew the line and explained that some people might drink one beer a day and think it's fine, while others go all out when they go out, which was me. I didn't drink every day, but she said, "You're one major life event away from losing complete control."

Remember the meaning behind the word addiction we talked about earlier? It comes from the Latin addictus, meaning "given over" or "bound." In essence, addiction is not just a habit—it is being surrendered, willingly or unwillingly, to something other than God.

I tested the boundaries of wisdom on my 30th birthday. I thought I could handle one drink while celebrating at a winery in Napa with friends. That was pride. One drink led to intoxication and foolish decisions, even though I was married with a young son. The Holy Spirit's conviction was immediate.

From that moment, I made a powerful choice: I surrendered that area of my life to Christ. Freedom followed. The same principle applied to coffee—remember my Starbucks 3x-a-day habit?—and even with sex. Before marriage, I was reckless and addicted to sex, and masturbation continued for a few years into my marriage.

Each time I faced these struggles, I chose to take off the old identity and walk in the newness of Christ. The old patterns lost their hold as I stepped into who God says I am.

So, if you're struggling in a certain area, let wisdom be your stepping stone to deliverance. Learn what's happening to your brain, your body, and your spirit. Pray through Romans 8. Surrender to the Holy Spirit. Remember: you always get to pick your hard.

Let me share a few simple daily practices that help redirect cravings and build new patterns centered on God:

- Start each day with a short prayer, asking God to fill your deepest needs and guide your cravings toward Him.

- Spend a few quiet minutes meditating on a scripture that reminds you of your new identity, like 2 Corinthians 5:17 or Romans 8:1.

- Keep a journal where you honestly record your thoughts, triggers, and victories. At the end of each entry, write down a gratitude or a promise from God's Word.

- When a craving hits, pause to breathe deeply and invite God into that moment. Whisper a simple prayer: "Jesus, I choose You to satisfy my soul."

- Share your journey with a trusted friend or support partner who can check in, encourage you, and pray with you regularly.

These small daily steps, repeated consistently, will help you replace old patterns with God's truth and develop life-giving habits. Even on the hardest days, you're forming a new story, one decision at a time.

Which is harder? Remaining in repetitive shame cycles, never truly filled, never satisfied? Or surrendering and allowing God's grace and mercy to fill you, giving you new clothes, new freedom, and a new trajectory? Often, that surrender doesn't just change your life—it changes the lives of generations to come.

If you find yourself slipping back into old patterns, do not lose hope. Setbacks happen, but they are not the end of your story. God's grace is always available to you. Instead of staying stuck in shame, return to Him—He welcomes you with open arms, again and again. Each time you turn back to Him, you are moving forward on the journey of healing and freedom.

Addiction is not your identity. Every time you choose God over anything else, you step further into the fullness of your true self—walking in freedom and abundance, clothed in Christ.

186

11

Chapter 11- Why Silence Keeps You Captive

When it comes to breaking free from captivity, silence can keep us bound. But there is a powerful act that sets us free: sharing our story. Sharing your testimony is more than just talking about what happened. It is a spiritual practice that literally undoes shame. In the Hebraic understanding, and in Scripture, speaking your story brings atonement. It opens the door for a new decree over your life.

Consider Mordechai and Esther. Their courage to reveal their true identities and speak up in a time of crisis brought redemption to an entire nation. This example shows that speaking truth in faith can create powerful change—not just for ourselves but for others as well. I experienced a taste of this after knee surgery, when I shared a deeply personal encounter with Jesus at my mentor's urging. Though I hesitated, that act of sharing lifted a heavy burden of shame from my life and brought new freedom.

Friends, you did it! You've reached the phase of pushing through—the step that propels you into complete healing. It's common to freeze or hold back here, but finishing the race requires stepping forward and sharing your story. Think of this as an evolving process: it can start small, and as you continue, it becomes more natural and empowering. The more you share, the more your endurance grows and you realize your soul was never meant to carry this story alone.

If you are wondering how to begin, start with small and safe steps. Try writing your story in a private journal, or recording a voice note just for yourself. When you feel ready, consider opening up to a trusted friend, mentor, or counselor—someone who will listen with kindness and respect. You might also look for a supportive small group where it is safe to share in community, even if it is just a few words at first. Each brave step helps you build confidence and trust in the process. Remember, you do not have to do it all at once. Let your journey unfold at a pace that honors where you are right now.

The primary impact of sharing your story is this: it breaks shame. When we keep trauma a secret, it creates a narrative in our mind, body, and soul that something about us is wrong. Sharing your story challenges that narrative. It's a spiritual act of truth-telling that realigns you with God's design and declares that your story matters. Shame often disguises itself in subtle ways—pushing past your boundaries or making you people-please. We can break this cycle by rejecting shame and honoring our unique design. Sharing our testimonies not only heals us but also empowers others to do the same.

In the Hebraic understanding, a testimony is more than just words. It is a declaration of what God has done in your life—a witness to His faithfulness. The Hebrew word for testimony, *edut*, comes from the root *ayin-dalet-vav-tav. This root* conveys the idea of standing as a witness and giving undeniable evidence.

When you speak your testimony, you declare the truth of God's work over your life and the events you have endured. This act of verbalizing truth pushes back against shame. Shame thrives in secrecy and silence, convincing us we are defective or unworthy. But when we testify—when we speak what is true about God's presence, provision, and redemption—we bring light into the darkness of shame. In Scripture, testimony often brings atonement and invites God's truth to replace lies. It breaks the power of shame over your mind, body, and spirit. Revelation 12:11 tells us, "They triumphed over him by the blood of the Lamb and by the word of their testimony; they did not love their lives so much as to shrink from death." This verse shows us that testimony is not just a personal declaration. It is a spiritual weapon. Speaking your story in faith breaks shame and aligns your voice with God's reality rather than the enemy's lies. Our testimony is both a shield and a sword: it breaks bondage, brings freedom, and creates a pathway for new blessings.

A psychologist observed that simply sharing trauma stories helps shift unhelpful beliefs without heavy therapeutic intervention. Reading one's trauma story aloud exposes and corrects false beliefs.

For example, a person who has been assaulted might believe they were targeted because of something inherent in themselves—"I'm an easy target"—when in reality, it may have been situational: wrong place, wrong time. By recounting what actually happened, the survivor begins to see that the trauma is not a reflection of personal failure or flaw, but rather a series of events that occurred beyond their control. Another powerful aspect of sharing our story is that each time we tell it, we desensitize the emotional and physical stress it carries. The more we share, the less triggering it becomes. And in our journey through this book, we now also have testimonies of our encounters with Jesus—from the Soul Delving chapter, when we prayed through the trauma and experienced His presence. Each time we share both the darkness and the light, we reinforce our healing and show how God has met us in the midst of pain.

Sharing your story also helps organize your life experiences. As you confront the trauma in your life, patterns begin to emerge: reactions, coping mechanisms, and sometimes even previously hidden events become clear. Recognizing these connections empowers you to create change and take control of your narrative. Remember, sharing your story is a powerful act—it sows seeds that will reap a harvest. Not everyone will be kind or believe you. Some may even reject or persecute you. Because of this, it is important to set healthy boundaries around your story and who you share it with. Start by choosing people you trust—those who have shown empathy, respect, and understanding. Ask yourself if you feel safe in their presence and whether they listen without judgment. It is okay to keep certain parts of your story private or to wait until you feel ready to share with a wider audience. You have permission to say no to uncomfortable situations or people who do not honor your story. Trust your sense of safety and give yourself grace to move at your own pace. I have experienced family members calling me a liar and harshly criticizing me, both online and in person. But these voices are not the truth. You are a daughter of Abba. You are known and loved by Him, and His truth defines your identity.

Romans 8:14-17 reminds us: "We have been adopted by God. The Spirit makes us sons and daughters of the Most High God. Because of this, we cry, 'Abba, Father.' We are heirs!"

Take a moment to let that sink in. You are an heir of God. You are set to inherit all that He has for you.

And remember Proverbs 19:23: when you live a life surrendered in love before God's law, you will experience abundant life, continual protection, and complete satisfaction.

Nobody can steal this from you. You have the power to replace every lie with the truth of your inheritance as God's daughter. As Colossians 2:10 reminds us: "And in Him you have been made complete, and He is the head over all rule and authority."

Nothing can truly complete you except Christ. On our own, we may strive for others' approval, but this is unrealistic because not everyone is living and operating in the Spirit. People can be mean, and sometimes the truth will make others uncomfortable.

When you face criticism or feel old patterns of shame resurfacing, here is a simple practice to help you stay grounded in your identity: each morning, take a few minutes to affirm who you are in Christ. You can choose one or two verses from the list that follows, speak them out loud over yourself, and thank God for making them true in your life. If you have a journal, write down your affirmations and any negative thoughts you notice so you can be intentional about replacing them with God's truth. You might also take a moment in prayer, inviting the Holy Spirit to remind you that your value is set by God, not by the opinions of others. Consistency in these small daily steps will help you grow stronger in truth and more resilient when challenges arise.

Your identity is secure as God's child. You do not need to earn love or strive for perfection. You are seen, known, and loved by your perfect Father, who welcomes all aspects of your story.

God invites us to experience heaven on earth. He will give you adventures that your soul craves, and He will always have your back. You can trust Him even if vindication hasn't yet appeared in the physical, because He is already working in the spiritual. He sees the beauty within you and is excited to partner with you in this life. So you never have to worry about missing exactly what God wants you to do or "missing your purpose." Your primary purpose is to be His beloved daughter; everything else will flow naturally as you co-live your life with Him. Purpose is not just about checking off devotionals or serving at church—it's about living every breath with Him in mind, talking to the Holy Spirit daily, and making Him part of the rhythm of your life. Before we end this book, I want to share a special experience that happened just recently. At the time, I wasn't sure why it happened—or why the timing was now—but after I went through the entire process, Abba revealed to me: *this is the end of your book.*

Let me paint the picture. It was a very cold, wintry, stormy day. I pulled into a gas station to get gas when a Facebook Marketplace notification lit up my screen. As I opened Facebook, right before my eyes appeared something I did not expect: a picture.It was a picture of a handsome, gentle-looking man with a young boy—and the moment I saw it, it hit me straight to my soul. I knew, in that instant, that this was my dad.

As you may remember from earlier in this book, my biological father is the one who abused me. The only pictures I had ever seen of him were two from my childhood—and they were dark, unkind images that reflected the trauma I carried. But this picture... This picture was different. And I was different too.I could feel the Spirit of God moving in my heart. A well of living water began to open inside me, and I could not stop crying. As the tears flowed, my body grew hotter and hotter. The presence of the Holy Spirit was on me, touching me so deeply. These were not tears of pain—they were tears of complete joy, happiness, love, and release.

In that moment, I could look at this man and feel love—love

like a child cherishes her parents. I am *not* suggesting that anyone should put themselves in close proximity to the person who abused them; my biological father is no longer living. But what I hope to leave you with is this: By applying the principles in this book, your soul can be healed. Your spirit can be freed. And one day, you can be so whole and free that you can look at the being who hurt you and feel love—not because of them, but because of the freedom God has brought you. You can rise. You can be whole. You can be free, my friend.

Friends, this is it! We are wrapping up the ARISE book, and I am so proud of you! If you feel like you need help sharing your story or navigating boundaries in your life, guidance is available. Whether it's navigating family dynamics, sharing your testimony, restoring intimacy in marriage, understanding healthy intimacy, praying through trauma, or learning to trust your body and mind, support is available to help you continue your journey. You can reach out to me directly for one-on-one coaching or mentorship, email me with your questions, or join our online community group where others are sharing and cheering each other on. For additional support, check the resources page in the back of this book for next steps. Do not hesitate to seek the help and encouragement you need—you are never alone, and there is a community here ready to support you.

Community is also essential in this season of your life. Surrounding yourself with people who understand, encourage, and celebrate your growth keeps you accountable and inspired. In a supportive community, you can share your testimony, hear others' stories, and continue to grow in healing and freedom.

I am excited to announce that I will be launching a new online community very soon. This space will offer group discussions, opportunities to share your story in a safe and supportive environment, and resources to keep your healing journey going. There will also be live Q&A sessions, prayer support, and workshops designed to help you deepen your faith and connect with others who truly understand your journey. If you are interested in joining, keep an eye on my socials and email updates for the official launch date and details on how to sign up. I would love for you to be part of this growing circle.

It has been a complete honor to share this book with you.

Please stay in touch, reach out when you need encouragement, and remember: if you ever feel stuck in any phase, you are not alone. Keep walking forward, keep speaking your story, and keep living as the beloved daughter of Abba who you truly are.

As we go, I want to speak this over you with boldness and authority:**You, my friend...**

You are redeemed, sanctified, and made righteous in Christ (1 Cor. 1:30).You have been transferred out of the kingdom of darkness and into the Kingdom of Light (Col. 1:13).

All your sins have been forgiven in Christ (Eph. 1:7).

You are a new creation—the old life has passed away completely (2 Cor. 5:17).

God has prepared good works in advance for you to walk in (Eph. 2:10).

You have become the righteousness of God in Christ (2 Cor. 5:21).

You overwhelmingly conquer in all things through Christ who loves you (Rom. 8:37).

You can do all things through Christ who strengthens you (Phil. 4:13).

God supplies all your needs according to His riches in glory (Phil. 4:19).

You are a child of God—deeply, eternally His (John 1:12; 1 John 3:1–2).

Your body is the temple of the Holy Spirit (1 Cor. 6:19).

It is no longer you who live, but Christ who lives in you and works through you (Gal. 2:20).

You have been delivered from Satan's authority—completely protected (Acts 26:18).

God's love has been poured into your heart by the Holy Spirit, blooming more every day (Rom. 5:5).

Greater is He who is in you than he who is in the world (1 John 4:4).

You are blessed with every spiritual blessing in the heavenly places (Eph. 1:3).

You are seated with Christ in the heavenly realms—far above every spiritual force; the enemy's intimidation is only a mirage (Eph. 2:4–6).

Because you love God and are called according to His purpose, He is working all things together for your good (Rom. 8:28).

If God is for you, who can be against you? No one. Their words carry no power because you are shielded by Him (Rom. 8:31).

Nothing can separate you from the love of Christ (Rom. 8:35–39).

All things are possible for you because you believe (Mark 9:23).

Because you are His child, God is leading you by His Spirit (Rom. 8:14).

As you follow the Lord, the path of your life grows brighter and brighter (Prov. 4:18).

God has given you special gifts to serve Him (1 Pet. 4:10–11).

You can cast out demons and lay hands on the sick, and they will recover (Mark 16:17–18).

God always leads you in triumph in Christ (2 Cor. 2:14).

You are an ambassador for Christ (2 Cor. 5:20).

You have eternal life (John 3:16).

Everything you ask in prayer, believing, you will receive (Matt. 21:22).

By Jesus' stripes, you are healed (1 Pet. 2:24).

You are an heir of God and a co-heir with Christ (Rom. 8:17).

You are part of a chosen race, a royal priesthood, a holy nation, and a people set apart for God (1 Pet. 2:9).

You are a member of the body of Christ (1 Cor. 12:27).

God will satisfy you with long life (Ps. 91:16).

Christ bore your sicknesses—including every wound, symptom, and aftermath of abuse—and carried your pain (Is. 53:4–5).

The Lord is your helper, so you will not fear (Heb. 13:6).

As you resist the devil, he flees from you (Jas. 4:7).

Your citizenship is in heaven, and heaven's resources can be called upon in your life (Phil. 3:20).

God will complete the good work He began in you (Phil. 1:6).

You have been redeemed from the curse of the law and every generational bondage—you have been adopted into His bloodline, and you inherit His benefits (Gal. 3:13).

12

Chapter 12: Resources

IT'S Your Turn
To Heal

Arise Community & Healing Journey

You were never meant to heal alone.

If this book has stirred hope in you, if parts of your story are beginning to come into the light, or if you sense the desire to walk your healing journey with others who understand, you are invited into the Arise Community.

This is a safe, faith-centered space where women heal together, grow together, and walk out freedom in real time.

Connected is Protected

10 Weeks- Journey to Healing — An Arise Group Journey

This 10-week small-group experience gently walks you through *Arise* week by week in community, with live coaching and support throughout the journey.

Together we:

- Process each chapter in a supportive circle
- Receive live weekly coaching and guidance
- Learn nervous system calming and regulation practices
- Share safely and confidentially
- Receive prayer and encouragement
- Practice practical steps toward peace
- Integrate healing at a sustainable pace

You are never pressured to share.

You are never rushed.

You are not alone.

Healing happens in connection, and this journey is designed to help you experience that truth.

Who This Is For

Women who:

- Desire healing from past wounds or trauma
- Feel stuck, anxious, or overwhelmed
- Long for peace in body, mind, and spirit
- Want safe Christian community
- Value guided support and coaching
- Are ready to walk through *Arise* with others

Whether you are just beginning or years into your healing journey, you are welcome here.

What You Can Expect

- Weekly live group sessions
- Live week-to-week coaching
- A structured path through *Arise*
- Trauma-aware, faith-based facilitation
- Community support between sessions
- Practical tools for daily life
- A compassionate, honoring environment

Join the Arise Community

To learn more or join the next Journey to Healing (10 Weeks to Peace) group, scan the code below. This will take you to a page with all the offers I have for you to help advance your healing journey.

The Arise Course

With the Arise Course, you have two options:

Option 1: Self-Paced Course
   Move through the Arise teachings at your own pace. You'll receive video teachings based on the book, along with guided activation to help you apply and embody what you're learning.

Option 2: Group Coaching Experience
   Join the group coaching program, which includes full access to the course plus live group coaching calls.

This is sacred, intentional time together. We heal in community.
   Connected is protected.

I have personally witnessed lifelong friendships form in these spaces as women rise, restore, and rebuild together.

Additional Offers

6-Week Healing from Trauma Intensive
   A powerful 6-week journey designed to help women heal deeply — not just emotionally, but within the nervous system and hormonal system as well.

The Legacy Arise Table
   A space where mothers come together to build spirit, body, and soul — which directly impacts their homes and businesses.
   Many women in this space step confidently into business, create financial abundance, and learn to live as their own brand.

You don't have to share your healing story here. This is for women ready for financial freedom and legacy-building.

Free Web Class

Learn how to create residual income and break cycles of lack and poverty.

Pain-Free & Peaceful Birth Blueprint

For my birthing moms — trauma does not get to steal your birth experience.

As a plus-size woman who had natural, pain-free births, I am passionate about equipping women with the tools, mindset, and nervous system regulation to birth in peace and power. You can find all offers at the qr code below, see you there!

IT'S Your Turn To Heal